Freedom to Learn

D1610297

The freedom of students to learn at university is being eroded by a performative culture that fails to respect their rights to engage and develop as autonomous adults. Instead, students are being restricted in how they learn, when they learn and what they learn by the so-called student engagement movement. Compulsory attendance registers, class contribution grading, group project work and reflective learning exercises based on expectations of self-disclosure and confession take little account of the rights of students or individual differences between them. This new hidden university curriculum is intolerant of students who may prefer to learn informally, are reticent, shy, or simply value their privacy. Three forms of student performativity have arisen – bodily, participative and emotional – which threaten the freedom to learn.

Key themes include:

- A re-imagining of student academic freedom
- The democratic student experience
- Challenging assumptions of the student engagement movement
- An examination of university policies and practices

Freedom to Learn offers a radically new perspective on academic freedom from a student rights standpoint. It analyzes the effects of performative expectations on students, drawing on the distinction between negative and positive rights to re-frame student academic freedom. It argues that students need to be thought of as scholars with rights and that the phrase 'student-centered' learning needs to be reclaimed to reflect its original intention to allow students to develop as persons. Student rights – to non-indoctrination, reticence, in choosing how to learn, and in being treated like an adult – ought to be central to this process in fostering a democratic rather than authoritarian culture of learning and teaching at university.

Written for an international readership, this book will be of great interest to anyone involved in higher education, policy and practice, drawing on a wide range of historical and contemporary literature related to sociology, philosophy and higher education studies.

Bruce Macfarlane is Professor of Higher Education at the University of Southampton, UK.

The Society for Research into Higher Education (SRHE) is an independent and financially self-supporting international learned Society. It is concerned to advance understanding of higher education, especially through the insights, perspectives and knowledge offered by systematic research and scholarship.

The Society's primary role is to improve the quality of higher education through facilitating knowledge exchange, discourse and publication of research. SRHE members are worldwide and the Society is an NGO in operational relations with UNESCO.

The Society has a wide set of aims and objectives. Amongst its many activities the Society:

• is a specialist publisher of higher education research, journals and books, amongst them Studies in Higher Education, Higher Education Quarterly, Research into Higher Education Abstracts and a long running monograph book series.

The Society also publishes a number of in-house guides and produces a specialist series "Issues in Postgraduate Education".

• funds and supports a large number of special interest networks for researchers and practitioners working in higher education from every discipline. These networks are open to all and offer a range of topical seminars, workshops and other events throughout the year ensuring the Society is in touch with all current research knowledge.

• runs the largest annual UK-based higher education research conference and parallel conference for postgraduate and newer researchers. This is attended by researchers from over 35 countries and showcases current research across every aspect of higher education.

SRHE *Society for Research into Higher Education*
Advancing knowledge Informing policy Enhancing practice

73 Collier Street
London N1 9BE
United Kingdom

T   +44 (0)20 7427 2350
F   +44 (0)20 7278 1135
E   srheoffice@srhe.ac.uk

www.srhe.ac.uk

Director: Helen Perkins
Registered Charity No. 313850
Company No. 00868820
Limited by Guarantee
Registered office as above

Society for Research into Higher Education (SRHE) series

Series Editor: Jennifer M. Case, University of Cape Town
Jeroen Huisman, University of Ghent

Freedom to Learn

The threat to student academic freedom and why it needs to be reclaimed

Bruce Macfarlane

Routledge
Taylor & Francis Group

LONDON AND NEW YORK

First published 2017
by Routledge
2 Park Square, Milton Park, Abingdon, Oxon OX14 4RN

and by Routledge
711 Third Avenue, New York, NY 10017

Routledge is an imprint of the Taylor & Francis Group, an informa business

© 2017 B. Macfarlane

British Library Cataloguing in Publication Data
A catalogue record for this book is available from the British Library

Library of Congress Cataloging in Publication Data
Names: Macfarlane, Bruce, 1961- author.
Title: Freedom to learn : the threat to student academic freedom and
    why it needs to be reclaimed / Bruce Macfarlane.
Description: Abingdon, Oxon ; New York, NY : Routledge is an
    imprint of the Taylor & Francis Group, an Informa Business,
    [2017] | Includes bibliographical references and index.
Identifiers: LCCN 2016009877 (print) | LCCN 2016021772 (ebook) |
    ISBN 9780415729154 (hbk : alk. paper) | ISBN 9780415729161
    (pbk : alk. paper) | ISBN 9781315529455 (ebk)
Subjects: LCSH: Academic freedom. | Education, Higher—Aims and
    objectives. | Student centered learning. | College students—
    Psychology.
Classification: LCC LC71 .M25 2017 (print) | LCC LC71 (ebook) |
    DDC 378.1/213—dc23
LC record available at https://lccn.loc.gov/2016009877

ISBN: 978-0-415-72915-4 (hbk)
ISBN: 978-0-415-72916-1 (pbk)
ISBN: 978-1-315-52945-5 (ebk)

Typeset in Galliard
by Swales & Willis Ltd, Exeter, Devon, UK

Printed and bound in Great Britain by
TJ International Ltd, Padstow, Cornwall

For my family, Yu-fen and Fiona,
and in memory of my mother
Brenda Macfarlane (née Whiteley) (1931–2014)

Contents

About the author

Bruce Macfarlane is professor of higher education at the University of Southampton, UK, and distinguished visiting professor at the University of Johannesburg, South Africa. He is a Fellow and former vice chair of the Society for Research into Higher Education and joint editor of *Policy Reviews in Higher Education*. His previous books with Routledge include *Intellectual Leadership in Higher Education* (2012), *Researching with Integrity* (2009), *The Academic Citizen* (2007) and *Teaching with Integrity* (2004).

Acknowledgments

This book has been a work in progress for a number of years and I am indebted to everyone who has offered me critical and constructive feedback during this period. I would like to thank Ravanne Lawday for her permission to reproduce parts of her blog that appear at the beginning of Chapter 5. I am also grateful to many academic colleagues with whom I have discussed this book or whose work I have engaged with substantively, including Ron Barnett, David Carless, Jenni Case, Lesley Gourlay, Tony Harland, Len Holmes, Thomas Karran, Manja Klemenčič, Roger Ottewill, Tristan McCowan, Jon Nixon and Jen Ross.

The ideas contained in this book have been the subject of a number of presentations and publications in journals and opinion pieces for the *Times Higher Education* and include:

Macfarlane, B. (2012) Be here now or else: lamentable consequences of student 'presenteeism', *Times Higher Education*, 13 December.
Macfarlane, B. (2012) Re-framing student academic freedom: a capability approach, *Higher Education*, 63, 6, 719–732.
Macfarlane, B. (2013) The surveillance of learning: a critical analysis of university attendance policies, *Higher Education Quarterly*, 67, 4, 358–373.
Macfarlane, B. (2014) Speaking up for the introverts, *Times Higher Education*, 25 September.
Macfarlane, B. (2014) Truly 'higher' study demands critical thinking, not faking it, *Times Higher Education*, 6 March.
Macfarlane, B. (2015) Student performativity in higher education: converting learning as a private space into a public performance, *Higher Education Research and Development*, 34, 2, 338–350.
Macfarlane, B. (2016) 'If not now, then when? If not us, who?' Understanding the student protest movement in Hong Kong. In R. Brooks (Ed.), *Student Politics and Protest: International Perspectives*. London and New York: Routledge.
Macfarlane, B. (2016) The performative turn in the assessment of student learning: a rights perspective, *Teaching in Higher Education*, doi: 10.1080/13562517.2016. 1183623

Introduction

My argument

The genesis of this book was an uncomfortable feeling that, despite all the emphasis in recent years on improving the student learning experience at university, and well-intentioned endeavors to make this experience more 'student-centered', something important has been forgotten. To me what appears to be missing is sufficient consideration of the rights of students and their freedom to learn.

Student academic freedom is usually thought of in terms of social and political activism. We are familiar with the idea of students protesting at what they perceive to be injustices, either at university or in civic society, and taking action such as organizing petitions, going on marches, occupying buildings on campus or taking other forms of non-violent direct action. Although it has its true historical origins in medieval times, this concept of student academic freedom is, in a Western context, one most often associated with the 1960s, a period of considerable social upheaval. Students found themselves at the forefront of protests during this turbulent period in respect to a variety of politically symbolic causes including campaigning against the Vietnam War, the nuclear arms race, the apartheid regime in South Africa, and, particularly in the United States, racial discrimination on campus and more widely in American society. During the time I have been writing this book, students around the world have been playing a leading role in high-profile political protest movements in places such as Chile, Taiwan and Hong Kong. Interpreting student academic freedom in this way is, of course, perfectly valid and still highly relevant today. The pro-democracy protests in Hong Kong in 2014 serve as an illustration of the way in which students can play a critical role in social and political movements. Universities ought to be important centers of critical conscience and students should be important actors in challenging the status quo and campaigning for a more just and equal society.

Yet, no matter how significant such campaigns may be, there is much more to student academic freedom than participating in social and political campaigns. I believe that there are other less visible, but nonetheless vital, ways in which student freedom needs to be more widely interpreted. These freedoms ought to be more deeply understood as being about how students learn at university: enjoying choice as adults in determining *when* they learn, *how* they learn and *what* they learn. What is important to point out here is that this interpretation of student freedom affects *all* students, not just the ones wishing to engage with social and political causes. Examples of what I mean by a student's freedom to learn – a phrase originally used by Carl Rogers (1969) – may principally be found in the way students are taught and assessed, both in the classroom and online.

Yet, our collective attention when it comes to teaching and assessment tends to be on educational effectiveness and efficiency rather than the extent to which this pedagogy supports a student's freedom to learn. Educational theorists who write about teaching and learning are mainly drawn from, or heavily influenced by, the field of psychology. Not surprisingly they often focus on the links between styles of teaching, learning and assessment, and the benefits in 'learning gain' that students derive from this process. These educationalists and researchers seek to measure the impact of different educational innovations. Their emphasis is currently very much about the extent to which approaches to teaching, learning and assessment might benefit from interventions that seek to increase 'student engagement' at university through active class participation, group and peer working, and policies that encourage, and more closely monitor, attendance at class.

The emphasis – and the justification – for these various interventions is ostensibly to improve the student 'learning experience'. The term 'learning gain' refers to evidence that students develop knowledge, skills and values relevant to employment, become less likely to drop out of their studies, do better in their exams and gain a good job when they graduate. Skills considered suitable for employment include being better able to interact with others or negotiating with peers as part of a group assignment. Student engagement policies further seek to shape student dispositions or attitudes, such as the importance of punctuality. This is one of the reasons given for compulsory attendance rules. The logic of student engagement policies might appear to be incontrovertible. Everyone is in favor of students succeeding both in their studies and in life after university, but ends do not always justify the means by which they are achieved.

There is an important thing missing here: sufficient consideration of the way in which such policies affect the rights of university students both as learners and as adult persons. There are various ways in which these changes in university policies and practices undermine the rights of students. In our collective eagerness to bring about learning gain, respond to the perceived expectations of employers and comfort ourselves that higher education represents good value for money for taxpayers, we seem to have forgotten that students are (in most contexts) adults and have freely chosen to be at university to learn. Given this reality it seems only logical and just that their freedom to learn in ways that meet their needs should be our paramount concern.

This freedom means that university students should not have things imposed on them that they do not want. Instead there should be a right to choose. This would include students being allowed to judge for themselves whether attendance at lectures and others classes constitutes value for their time. Lectures should not be compulsory. Students should have the right to learn in ways that meet their needs and dispositions as persons. Here, I believe that the distinction often drawn between 'passive' as opposed to 'active' learning has become an over-simplified dualism that has led to the vilification of students who prefer to study in an undemonstrative manner, often on their own and in silence. Even reading, an activity traditionally core to advanced learning, has been labeled pejoratively as 'passive'. Student engagement policies and practices promote 'active' learning as an essential means of evidencing learning. Yet, relying on observation is a crude means of understanding the complexity of how students learn and engage. It further distorts patterns of student behavior that are altered to satisfy such requirements. Performative expectations such as attending classes, showing an 'enthusiasm' for learning or demonstrating emotions such as 'empathy' through a self-reflective exercise are all non-academic achievements. They are merely behavioral demands that students are expected to conform with.

In this book I use the word 'performative' as a description of these increasing demands. It refers to things that can easily be observed and measured and is based on a simplistic behavioral approach to understanding learning. I use this word as the student is forced to act out a given behavior or emotion in a way which is both manipulative and inauthentic. It requires the student to behave in a manner or to espouse beliefs that will satisfy such demands. Students must expend their energies being compliant and potentially fake certain prescribed attitudes or values. Such demands have nothing to do with the core purpose of a real higher education which should be about learning and interrogating claims to knowledge and truth in an environment that promotes freedom and personal autonomy.

Mea culpa

My own journey to the position I argue for in this book has taken place over the course of my academic career since the late 1980s, during which time I have worked in universities in the UK and in Hong Kong. To be honest, during this time I have practiced or promoted many of the teaching and assessment strategies which seem to me now, with the benefit of hindsight, to have potentially negative consequences for student academic freedom. I have come to the position I am advocating in this book after working for 28 years in the higher education sector. This does not mean I am necessarily wiser, but I now look at things from a different angle.

As a teacher I have always prided myself on deploying a range of strategies for getting students actively engaged in their learning. I have never been an advocate of anything else. But in so doing I have become increasingly uncomfortable with compelling participation in group processes and assessing such contributions. As a business and management lecturer during the 1980s and 1990s I made extensive use of group work assessment. Like most of my colleagues, I used to tell students who complained about what they perceived as the unfairness of allocating groups a common grade that this simply reflected the reality of working life.

I now think this analogy is flawed and, moreover, represents one of the most frequently practiced injustices visited on higher education students. I also used to be an enthusiastic proponent of assessing students' reflective learning logs as part of a business ethics course in which they wrote about the way in which their values and assumptions had been reshaped by the course (Macfarlane, 2001). I now feel that such forms of assessment often constitute an invasion of privacy and make unreasonable demands on students to enter into what has been termed a confessional discourse (Fejes and Dahlstedt, 2013). Finally, as an academic developer at three different UK universities for 10 years from 2000, I advocated a range of active learning strategies without regard to the negative impact of these approaches on student academic freedom. So it's a case of *mea culpa*!

I have become particularly concerned about the way the phrase 'student-centered' has become an educational mantra synonymous with compulsory participation in class. It seems to me that we now too readily accept that 'active' learning is good for everyone. As I explain in the book, the founding father of student-centered learning, Carl Rogers, always emphasized the need to respect the right of students to make their own decisions about whether to participate in class. Unfortunately, Rogers' ideas connected with student-centered learning appear to have been hijacked to suit institutional imperatives that punish students who do not comply with the principles of student performativity in the university. Students who resist or fail to comply with student engagement policies are negatively labeled as 'feral' and 'passive' learners or online 'lurkers'. Some students – Western as well as Asian – are simply shy. It seems ironic that, in an educational culture that emphasizes respect for diversity as an article of faith, we now vilify students who prefer to learn in a private space rather than in a more public, performative space.

My personal experience as a university professor working in Hong Kong during the student-led democracy protests in 2014 made me realize that conventional ways of thinking about student academic freedom in terms of the right to protest and participate in politics and university affairs is closely connected with freedom to learn in the classroom. During this time many undergraduates participated in the Occupy Central movement to demand the right for the people of Hong Kong to choose their own leader as a constituent part of the People's Republic of China but one with its own unique colonial, cultural and linguistic heritage (Macfarlane, 2016). Many universities in Hong Kong during this time continued to take attendance registers, something which I regard, in any case, as counter-intuitive to the voluntary nature of a higher education. But the taking of attendance registers during a period of student protest in an undemocratic political system raises serious concerns about how such information may be used both at the time absences are recorded and in the future. This is why I personally lobbied the vice chancellor to suspend the use of attendance registers at the University of Hong Kong.

This book sets out to challenge the assumptions that underpin the way modern universities define what it means to be student-centered and, in so doing, offers a reimagining of student academic freedom beyond its conventional associations with student protest movements. Instead, I argue, it needs to be understood in terms of freedom to engage in higher education on a voluntary basis and according to individual learning preferences. Using such things as attendance registers or class contribution grading or requiring compliance with normative values about world politics (e.g. global citizenship) are not conducive to student academic freedom. These things introduce restrictions, and soft forms of indoctrination, rather than freedoms. The freedom to learn needs to be understood as both as a negative right not to have certain liberties taken away from students and as a positive right to enable them to exercise freedoms that will promote their personal growth as independent thinkers.

I am not against all use of active learning or student engagement in the life of the university or wider society. However, I am arguing that these ideas should not be imposed on all students and that student engagement needs to be constructed in a democratic manner that places choice and voluntarism at the heart of the student experience. There is a need to truly respect students as learners rather than demanding compliance with a set of performative expectations that often require students to act in a way that is inauthentic and does not enable them to develop independence and maximize their choices.

This book is dedicated to the memory of my mother, Brenda Macfarlane. She was someone who gained a place to study at Liverpool University in the late 1940s but, like a lot of women of her generation, never got the chance to take up this opportunity. Despite this, my mother taught me a lot about the freedom to learn. When I was a young boy, more interested in playing football and reading comics than in books or formal learning, she never put me under any pressure. She understood that everyone has to find their own way and that ultimately the freedom to learn is about an individual choice and respecting different forms of 'engagements', in the language of our time. Carl Rogers had a phrase for it: 'freedom from pressure' (1951: 395).

In writing this book I hope I will be able to prompt a debate about how to better balance what is in the interests of students from both a *learning* and a *rights* perspective and to challenge some of the assumptions of the student engagement movement that are rapidly becoming received wisdom across global higher education.

Chapter 1

The hidden curriculum

What is needed is a new academic professionalism based upon a more generous and expansive notion of academic freedom as *freedom for others*: the responsibility of academics to ensure that others have the responsibility to speak their own minds, to learn in accordance with their own interests, and to enjoy a secure framework within which to learn.

(Nixon *et al.*, 1998: 278)

Introduction

I believe that the freedom of students to learn at university is under threat. By this I mean that the right of students to develop and learn as they wish as autonomous adults is being seriously undermined. Ironically, while students have never been as free to make choices in the way they conduct their private lives as adults, they have never been as *unfree* to learn at university in the ways in which they might prefer. The book will seek to substantiate this claim and outline what can be done to reassert the centrality of student academic freedom in terms of the 'freedom to learn' at university.

First, I will contend that university students are now subject to participative, behavioral and emotional expectations that inhibit the development and expression of their academic freedom. These expectations treat university students as children rather than adults and the extent to which they can genuinely develop as independent learners is restricted as a result. What I call *student performativity* will be illustrated by reference to requirements that students publicly demonstrate the way in which they are learning through a regime of participative processes (participative performativity, see Chapter 5), the growth of an attendance culture at university (bodily performativity, see Chapter 6), and the increasing importance attached to the sharing of personal feelings and emotions in learning and assessment practices, including the espousal of certain politically correct values (emotional performativity, see Chapter 7). These three forms of performativity constitute a hidden curriculum that the contemporary university student needs to navigate and represents a serious undermining of their freedom to learn.

The phrase 'hidden curriculum' is one originally coined by Philip Jackson (1968) to refer to the ways that schools socialize pupils by rewarding them for complying with certain dispositions, values and behavioral norms such as waiting quietly, keeping busy, being respectful toward teachers, and generally being cooperative, courteous and punctual (Jackson 1968: 10–33). In a higher education context the hidden curriculum may be understood as a set of social rules and academic conventions that both teachers and students learn in order to survive and succeed (Bennett *et al.*, 2004). Conventionally, this is interpreted in terms of acquiring social capital and rote and surface learning techniques to pass examinations. Yet it is now increasingly represented by a different kind of performative game in which students need to be able to understand and respond to a changed set of professorial assumptions and values (Snyder, 1971). The values and behaviors expected of students in a contemporary higher education context may be a little different than those expected of school children during the 1960s but the process of socialization that Jackson identified is still occurring. Some aspects of the new hidden curriculum at university, such as the emphasis now placed on punctuality and compulsory attendance at classes, look very similar to those originally associated with schooling by Jackson, while other elements, such as the stress now placed on active participation in the higher education classroom, represent the way some conventional expectations have been turned on their head.

Second, I will argue that university students should primarily be regarded as novice scholars, not as 'customers'. They are autonomous adults who have chosen to further their education at university for a variety of reasons. Yet their primary identity as novice scholars is being submerged beneath a new identity as a managed customer, one of several so-called stakeholders that higher education institutions seek to satisfy and placate. Ironically, beyond the rhetoric and marketing hype, this identity weakens rather than strengthens the rights of students as learners. They are domesticated, or made docile, in their roles as managed 'customers' and subject to constraints as learners rather than as adult members of an academic community. While it is popular to contend that students enjoy heightened rights as customers, the reality is that their rights as student members of an academic community are in retreat. It is not just students who face performative demands though. These are also encountered by what I call the *performative university*. This phrase is used as a shorthand to describe the way that the values of higher education institutions are now shaped by the instrumentalism of governments that increasingly view education, and especially higher education, in terms of a preparation for employment.

Finally, in response to these trends, I outline how student academic freedom can be re-claimed. I will initially demonstrate how academic freedom has long been interpreted as an exclusive, self-regarding privilege of the professoriate. In rebalancing matters I will outline how student rights need to be understood as about building the capacity of learners. This will draw on an approach derived from the work of Amartya Sen (1999) and others such as Martha Nussbaum (2003) in urging a focus on the development of positive 'capabilities' in students.

Such an approach can help refocus our understanding of student academic freedom as about capacity building. A series of student rights will be identified which I believe can help restore the importance of student academic freedom, respecting their adulthood and enabling them to develop as independent learners. This is, in a nutshell, my argument. Hopefully, what follows in the book will help to convince you, the reader.

Student academic freedom

There is a voluminous literature about academic freedom. If you type the phrase 'academic freedom' into the internet search engine Google it results in millions of hits. Numerous articles, websites, university policy statements and discussion forums focus on issues relating to the rights of academic faculty working in universities around the world to free expression and enquiry. By contrast, the phrase 'student academic freedom' produces around three times fewer hits. One might conclude from this quick and crude comparison that there is three times more interest in academic freedom for faculty members than for students but on closer inspection the difference is even starker. The vast majority of web links referencing student academic freedom as a search term tend to relate to the generic concept and seldom, if ever, refer to students in any detail whatsoever.

This simple search illustrates a key point: the study of academic freedom rarely connects with the freedom of students. Instead, it focuses on freedom for academic faculty. Academics who write about academic freedom are largely writing about the importance of a protection that they assert *for themselves* (e.g. Nelson, 2010). The literature is, in essence, self-referential. Indeed the rights of academics are taken as more or less synonymous with the concept of academic freedom. A number of books about academic freedom fail to mention students at all (e.g. Russell, 1993). It is almost as if academics have forgotten that students are also members of the academic community. Or, perhaps, the truth is that they do not regard them as such. As I hope to make plain in what follows, the neglect of student academic freedom is an oversight that needs correcting.

Conventionally, where student academic freedom is characterized it is in terms of students being represented in the governance of an academic institution and in being allowed to freely protest and publicly campaign on issues of concern to them. The student radicalism on campuses in the 1960s might be seen as a high point of student academic freedom on the basis of this interpretation. Threats to student academic freedom have tended to be interpreted as censorship in the classroom or students feeling too intimidated to voice any opinion contrary to that of their professor (Weber, 1973a; Horowitz, 2002; AAUP, 2007). This is called self-censorship and is a concern I will consider in the chapter that follows (see Chapter 2).

I want to approach student academic freedom from a fresh angle, one that is a little different from these previous interpretations. Instead of thinking of it as someone being *prevented* from speaking freely I will seek to analyze what needs to be done to *enable* students to fully enjoy their academic freedom. Put another way, students need to be afforded the *capability* to be free. This is more than a semantic point and requires an approach based on positive as well as negative rights. Well-known examples of positive rights include the right to education, basic health care and employment. Positive rights are generally associated with a more radical agenda for change in society. Adopting a positive rights perspective is partly about shifting the language. Rather than thinking about what students should have *freedom from*, we should focus on what they ought to have *freedom to*. It is a more action-oriented approach and necessitates steps to be taken to bring about student academic freedom. In other words, it is inadequate to baldly state that students are not prevented from freely expressing their ideas.

Student performativity

I am advocating a positive agenda to help students develop and realize their capabilities (Nussbaum, 2003) and to gain the necessary self-confidence to fulfil their potential as learners and as thinkers. Few would probably disagree with this sentiment but there are significant barriers in practice preventing the achievement of this goal. The first is embodied in the phrase 'student performativity'. This refers to the way that students are evaluated on the basis of how they learn – and are *seen to learn* – at university. Conventionally this might be taken as meaning passing their in-course assessments or final examinations.

Here, though, I am referring to a much broader set of expectations about the way students are expected to behave, demonstrate their commitment to participate in class, to assessment practices involving their peers or involving personal 'confession', and to an enthusiastic adherence to certain values associated with the contemporary university. There are values long associated with student learning in a liberal higher education such as tolerance of the opinions of others or openness to criticism (Barnett, 1990). These are essential to the functioning of learning in a liberal university. Yet, there are now further expectations associated with performativity that go well beyond co-operating with the basic conditions necessary for higher learning. These demand that students show evidence of their learning that can be easily audited as it occurs in the public space of the classroom or online forum. Such expectations have become an integral part of university life, justified by the student engagement movement in terms of evidencing the time and effort which students put into their studies and the benefits they are said to derive from doing so. Such demands represent a natural extension of the audit culture identified by Michael Power (1994, 1997) and others and threaten student autonomy, privacy and learning diversity in the sense of students being allowed to choose how they prefer to engage as learners. This represents an important part of my argument and demonstrates the way that learning at university has changed over the last 20 years or so.

The phrase 'student performativity' may be new to readers who may be more familiar with the term 'teacher performativity' (Ball, 2003, 2012). This refers to the world of targets, evaluations and performance indicators that apply to schoolteachers and university professors. In a higher education context, individual academics encounter a range of measures that purportedly measure the quality of their performance. These include research audits assessing their research publications, course experience questionnaires evaluating the quality of their teaching, and income generation targets. The mantras are about 'teaching excellence' and 'world-class research'. The latter is often narrowly characterized as about publishing in high impact international journals on the basis of research funded by prestigious grant-awarding bodies. In complying with such demands, academics need to do so in word as well as deed. It requires a casting aside or suppression of personal views and demands a 'playing of the game'. This implies, among other things, publishing early and often in the research cycle even when this might be at the expense of longer-term goals and teaching responsibilities. Working in a performative environment leads to inauthentic attitudes and behavior as individuals endeavor to conform to such expectations. In research terms it results in a move away from certain types of publication outputs such as books or book chapters, less willingness to undertake service activities for the benefit of the wider academic community, and increasing rates of research grant applications and publication output in international journals. Those who try to resist by refusing to 'play the game', by not adjusting their behavior toward the goals and targets set, are punished by failing to gain promotion, being moved onto a teaching-only contract or losing out in other, more subtle ways, in an increasingly competitive and performative academic culture (Lucas, 2006).

Student performativity is simply the mirror image of teacher performativity. It is just the targets and the performance indicators that differ. The performative demands typically include attending classes punctually, taking part in classroom discussions in order to convey an impression of enthusiasm and commitment, participating in group work and peer evaluation exercises, posting comments to online learning forums, and displaying or espousing the 'right' attitudes, such as being committed to 'global citizenship'. Learning to conform to this set of expectations is an integral part of what it now means to be a university student. This hidden curriculum involves students (and their professors, to some extent) taking part in a ritual of inauthenticity. Lip service is paid to certain elements of the teaching regime, such as the espousal of learning 'outcomes', but, in practice, there is limited belief in their veracity. They are simply things that everyone needs to (pretend to) comply with. Those students who do not comply with the performative regime are castigated, and negatively labeled as 'social loafers' or online 'lurkers'. Those discontent with the way in which an individual grade might have been awarded on the basis of a group work project are dismissed as 'grade grubbers'. Legitimate complaints about a lack of fairness in assessment are condemned as an indicator of rising levels of consumerism among the student population.

The series of behaviors which university students are required to perform in modern higher education have parallels with the world of reality television. Here, contestants compete with each other through their bodily, participative and emotional performance (Skeggs, 2009). They do this, for example, by displaying emotions such as guilt, shame and passion. Many of these programs are premised on the notion of self-transformation. The obese learn how to live a healthier lifestyle and face the reasons why they overeat; hoarders learn how to de-clutter their homes and emotionally let go of their possessions; the poorly dressed are taught how to select clothes that improve their appearance and deal with issues of low esteem in the process. These television programs are not only about cooking, house clearing and 'lifestyle'. They are more subtly about the public display of emotions. Participants go through an emotional journey that leads them to become 'better' or more emotionally self-aware people. There are messages here about self-worth, social class and what it means to be a 'good' person demanding loquaciousness and emotional openness in talking about one's own feelings.

The terminology used by Beverley Skeggs (2009) has resonance in higher education. *Bodily performativity* occurs in the sense that students are required to attend class or face punishment in assessment grading and emotional pressure where non-attendance is interpreted as a personal affront to the ego of the professor. A *participative performativity* is about a willingness to conform to learning regimes that emphasize active participation and assessment in peer groups. Finally, *emotional performativity* is connected with being prepared to conform to a set of values sanctified by the institution and represented through the written and unwritten curriculum. Examples include a desire to be a 'global citizen', possess intercultural understanding or espouse the importance of 'reflexivity' in professional practice. Here there is an expectation that higher education is a personally transformative process that makes a positive contribution to wider society. This is a laudable goal but is inappropriate in developing higher education students as independent learners with the right to make their own choices about what to believe in. It imposes a particular view of the world on students. Hence, it is clear that learning at university is being influenced in ways that increasingly mirror the expectations of reality television. If you think that the analogy between reality television and learning at university is far-fetched, consider, for example, the way in which class or audience response systems are now deployed in higher education classrooms to compel reluctant students to participate (Graham *et al.*, 2007). Such systems do not just provide a means by which students may engage; they build in an expectation as part of the process of socialization. The public sharing or display of certain dispositions, values and emotions is the signature feature of this hidden curriculum.

Engagement and ideology

Some readers might wonder what is wrong with expectations that students ought to attend class, participate and demonstrate a preparedness to make a positive contribution to the world in response to its problems. Indeed, there is a growing body of literature about *student engagement* that advocates its benefits. This phrase is widely invoked in international higher education circles evidenced by an increasing number of academic papers, books and university policy initiatives. It implies a learning environment where participants, drawn from diverse backgrounds, are actively engaged in a participatory culture and experience an adequately resourced and interactive approach to teaching (Newswander and Borrego, 2009; Fredricks *et al.*, 2004; Haworth and Conrad, 1997: 553).

The conceptual basis for this belief is connected to the work of thinkers and educational psychologists such as John Dewey, Jean Piaget, Lev Vygotsky and Carl Rogers. They believed that learning should be an active and social process. Sometimes this is described as it being child-centered or, in a higher education context, student-centered. Their argument was that the individual autonomy of the learner should be at the heart of education and this should be centered on the needs and interests of the child or adult learner.

In a higher education context, the work of Carl Rogers (1951, 1969) has probably been the most highly influential in establishing the term student-centered. In explaining the term Rogers identified many of the principles with which educators in higher education are familiar today: creating a permissive and non-judgmental environment, promoting individual and group discussion, recasting the teacher as a facilitator and encouraging students to self-evaluate (Rogers, 1951). Yet crucially, Rogers' position was premised on the principles of freedom and democracy. He argued that students should be 'free from pressure' (1951: 395) and make their own choices about how they wished to learn, including whether to attend class, to contribute to discussions or stay silent, and to learn actively or passively.

Dewey, Piaget, Vygotsky and Rogers argued that the purpose of education was a democratic one and that learning is a social process in which people construct meaning based on an interaction between their own experience and ideas. Constructivism is often used as a catch-all term to describe these ideas that have been widely interpreted as supporting classroom learning where students benefit from active and collaborative approaches as opposed to ones that rely on direct instruction or the 'transmission', or one-way delivery, of knowledge by the teacher. This has set up a series of popular but misleading dualisms between constructivism and direct instruction; between student-centered and teacher-centered; and between active and passive learning. In common with most dualisms, these all imply that one of the two approaches is inferior as well as morally suspect. You will find few educationalists defending direct instruction, being teacher-centered or promoting student learning which is passive although there are those who argue that the claims of learning approaches that use minimal guidance have been exaggerated in terms of their overall effectiveness (Kirschner *et al.*, 2006).

Enthusiasm for an approach to teaching based on the principles of constructivism has led to a narrow and dogmatic interpretation of this theory of learning.

Understanding learning as a social process does not *exclude* approaches to learning that are often labeled as passive, such as reading or solitary reflection, where an individual is interacting with the ideas of another presented in a written text or based on their own ideas and observations. While constructivism has implications for teaching, it is really a theory about learning and so does not disqualify approaches such as lectures. It is a myth that constructivism implies that students should always be learning in an active and reflective way (Clements, 1997). The distinction drawn between deep learning and surface learning has come to represent a 'right' and a 'wrong' way for students to learn (Howie and Bagnall, 2013). It represents an accusation that students are failing to engage properly with the subject or discipline and merely doing enough to get by or pass an examination. The dichotomy between being 'student-centered' and 'teacher-centered' leveled at the teacher is similarly censorious. Being 'teacher-centered' implies that a teacher is failing to put the needs of their students before their own, perhaps egotistical interests; it is a disparagement that the teacher cares more about themselves than their own students.

The dichotomies referred to above are now firmly entrenched in the lexicon of higher education pedagogy. 'Student-centered', 'deep learning' and 'active learning' have taken on the status of sacred pedagogical slogans. There is a growing pragmatic agenda supporting the use of active learning involving peer group learning and assessment in particular. Getting students to work in groups and assess the product of their joint endeavors is often designed as an efficient way of handling rising numbers of students in university classes. It can be seen as a way of reducing the time and effort involved in assessing the work of each individual student. This reality is too often masked by the mantra of active learning. The language of graduate employability is another element of this pragmatic and largely instrumental agenda supporting active and group processes in student learning and assessment. The claimed benefits of student engagement include reductions in university drop-out rates, better examination results and learners who are better prepared for the labor market (e.g. Allen, 1999; Astin, 1993; Kuh *et al.*, 2008). Student engagement appears to be a no-brainer – a good idea all round, offering something on which both educational theorists and policy makers can agree. To question it might seem perverse.

So why am I questioning it? My problems with the assumptions that lie behind the mantra of student engagement are threefold. First, there is a focus largely on how students *act* or *perform* rather than what they *know*. Such expectations are essentially about seeking to get students to conform to the behavioral rules of the hidden curriculum such as looking enthusiastic in class, being willing to participate, or appearing sympathetic toward fashionable social or political orthodoxies. Second, the demand for students to 'engage' fails to respect a student's right to learn in the way in which they choose. It dictates the manner of this engagement as being social, group-based and about oral loquaciousness. Third, advocates of student engagement seem to have forgotten that higher education is about knowledge, no matter how provisional and potentially contentious, as well as about skills and attitudes. Legislating that students should have certain types of attitudes or hold particular values is not a liberating approach to education. If, on the other hand, students can engage with knowledge, both in its propositional and its professional forms, this is ultimately far more liberating as students are given the freedom to decide what to do with and how to interpret this knowledge for themselves. It is their choice to make up their own minds about what to believe in. This is the basis of what Karl Popper (1945) called an 'open society'.

Instead, learning at university is fast becoming, to use the words of Christopher Lasch (1979), about the 'performing self'. Why should learning be a public rather than a private process? Surely individuals should have the right to learn in the way they choose? It further depends on how words such as 'participation' or 'engagement' are interpreted. Institutions tend to interpret these words quite narrowly to refer to easily observable behavior, such as attendance at class and oral contributions in class discussion. However, this excludes behavior often negatively labeled as 'passive', such as listening skills or private reflection. Learning is a private as well as a public process. Freedom to learn implies a right to reticence as well as a right to speak.

Higher education should not simply be understood as a continuation of compulsory schooling. It is a voluntary process connected more with the critical questioning of knowledge claims rather than the simple acquisition of texts and the inculcation of certain skills and attitudes (Barnett, 1990). The claims of student engagement reflect a wider moral panic in society that students are not engaging or participating enthusiastically enough while at university, that they need to engage more in ways that can be evidenced, and that this evidence should be collected to show that this is happening in order to demonstrate that institutions are meeting their obligations to wider society. At the heart of this moral panic are worries that higher education is not offering sufficient value for money. Evidence about student 'engagement' is meant to assuage these concerns.

Anxieties about the extent of student engagement are based on false assumptions that university students should be 'in love with' their subject and committed to a life that revolves around an outdated and elitist model of what it means to be a student. Members of the professoriate that support student engagement policies are guilty of a Golden Ageism that students of past generations were more intrinsically motivated, seeing learning as an end in itself, and more passionate about their subject than contemporary students. The evidence to support this belief is, at best, inconclusive (see Chapter 5). The idea that students need to be somehow coerced into engagement at university is further based on the outdated assumption that learners are all young, immature individuals who are studying full-time and are able to immerse themselves entirely in their studies. It ignores the reality of mass higher education that a large proportion of students are over the age of 25 years old, work full- or part-time and may not regard their identity as a student as the most important thing in their life. These other identities – employee, mother, father, carer, volunteer and so on – may play a more significant role in their life than being a student.

The performative university

Student performativity is about what happens at the micro level, in the classroom or online forum. It concerns how students are taught and assessed, and how these processes can potentially undermine the extent to which they can develop their autonomy in *when*, *how* and *what* they learn. Yet the threats to student academic freedom go deeper and wider. Institutions are themselves subject to performative expectations. These stem from governments keen to extract what they regard as better value for money in return for public spending on higher education. Such pressures derive from other sources such as influential donors and sponsors of university research. There is now an international market for higher education, especially among more research-oriented institutions, symbolized by the emergence in recent years of global university rankings. These include Academic Ranking of World Universities (or Shanghai Jiao Tong index) and the QS (Quacquarelli Symonds) World University Rankings. On a national basis, there are a host of other ranking tables, such as Poland's Perspektywy University Ranking, as institutions vie for prestige and a slice of the market locally, nationally, regionally and globally.

The demands on the performative university directly affect students in a number of ways. First, students, it is now claimed, are customers. Writing in a predominantly UK context, Clouder and Hughes (2012: 1) claim that 'the advent of student fees is promoting a consumer culture in which students are becoming "customers" with an increasingly powerful voice in shaping curricula to their own requirements.' This statement carries the implication that student concerns, interests and needs are addressed in a more efficient and business-like way. Actually, the opposite is true. The reality is that students are now treated *worse* than customers. This is because the deepening acceptance of this analogy has stripped from them their primary identity as novice members of a scholarly community. Instead they are 'managed customers' with universities as keen to exploit the results of student evaluation data for their marketing and communication strategy as to apply the results to bring about genuine self-improvement at the program level. The so-called 'student voice' is largely used as a rhetorical catchphrase by universities keen to impress on others the extent to which they involve students in academic affairs. While this phrase is understood in the school sector as about student rights and involvement in governance, the purpose of most 'student voice' projects in a higher education context tends to be about either quality enhancement or professional development (Seale, 2010). Although the use of this phrase might give the impression that institutions have the best interests of students at heart, such initiatives domesticate the student voice within university quality assurance structures while selling the benefits that they can gain as student representatives in terms of employment-related skills, thereby encouraging a process of self-commodification (see Chapter 3).

Contemporary universities need to be all things to all people (Parker and Crona, 2012). They seek to respond ever more keenly to the needs and expectations of a wide range of stakeholders, notably governments, employers, professional bodies, parents and donors. It is increasingly these organizations and interest groups, rather than students, who are the *real* customer. Programs have developed in conjunction with, or specifically for, large and influential public or business organizations, such as in-company MBAs (master's in business administration), and other programs sponsored by private and public sector organizational consortia with similar needs have grown considerably over the last 30 years in response to market demand. The students tend to be mature-aged middle managers undertaking postgraduate or post-experience study and often looking for opportunities to further their career within – or possibly outside of – the sponsoring organization. These students, who have another identity as employees of the same organization, are the consumers but the real customer is the sponsoring organization. Not unnaturally, the curriculum reflects the interests and priorities of the customer rather than the student-as-consumer. This has implications for the extent to which it serves the interest of participants who may well have plans that are not restricted to working for the sponsoring organization for the rest of their career. In-company programs do not only fundamentally alter the relationship between students and the university. They alter the classroom environment. In classes where students are exclusively drawn from the same organization this can have a potentially negative effect on freedom of expression since discussion takes place in an environment with workplace peers (and possibly superiors) rather than with peers drawn from a variety of other organizations (Macfarlane, 2000). Workplace relations and politics become part of, rather than separate from, the learning environment in the corporate classroom. In short, academic freedom is limited in partnerships between corporations and public universities (Blass, 2001). The effect on student academic freedom of single organization or 'in-company' programs is just one example of the way in which the relationship between students and the university is being undercut. This book will explore the hollowness of the student-as-customer analogy in a range of further ways, including the way in which universities are treating students as if they were 'employees' by claiming ownership of their intellectual property rights (see Chapter 8). Here, students are victims of a culture that is both corporate and patriarchal.

Conclusion

Understanding of student academic freedom is central to a democratic and emancipatory higher education that genuinely places the students at the heart of the learning process. Protecting student rights as learners should be the primary consideration of university learning and teaching strategies but the expectations of student performativity, often justified on the basis of educational dogmas about active learning and learning 'gain' to meet the needs of the employability agenda, dominate current thinking and classroom practice. In this book I will argue for the need to redefine what is meant by student-centered by focusing on the freedom and autonomy of the learner, drawing on principles derived from Carl Rogers and the independent learning movement. These rights act as a way of reclaiming the phrase student-centered that needs to be understood as about fostering a democratic rather than authoritarian culture of learning and teaching at university. The student rights that I will identify – to non-indoctrination, reticence, in choosing how to learn and in being treated like an adult – should play a much more significant role in the way that student learning is understood. The chapters that follow will expand on the issues raised above, by developing this line of argument further.

Chapter 2

Student rights

'Can't I exist, as well?'

Malcolm Bradbury's satirical campus novel The History Man *is centered on the life and loves of a fictional character by the name of Dr. Howard Kirk, a radical sociologist who embraces free love, a classless society and a Marxist world-view. Kirk is a caricature of the left-wing lecturer of his day, a politically outspoken and intolerant ideologue as well as a rogue in his private life. The novel is set during the so-called 'permissive' society of the early 1970s, a period following shortly after the social revolution of the late 1960s. It subtly questions some of the assumptions and contradictions of these times from a liberal humanist perspective. In the early 1980s, when the book was dramatized for British television, it became emblematic of all that was perceived to be wrong with UK universities in its characterization of academic life at a time when the Conservative government of Margaret Thatcher had started to radically reform the higher education sector. The book was even blamed for the decline of sociology as a subject at university.*

In the book, Howard Kirk is shown to be an intellectual bully who demands that his students agree with his Marxist view of the world. One of Kirk's students is a young man who dresses in a manner out-of-step with the informality of the age. Rather than wearing the emerging uniform of the classless society, a pair of jeans and a T-shirt, he sports a university blazer and a tie more reminiscent of student dress during the 1950s, a time despised by Kirk for its fustiness, conservatism and rigid class divisions. Compared with his classmates, the young man appears to hold conservative political views much to the annoyance of Kirk who proceeds to take out his intolerance of any traces of non-Marxist thinking by repeatedly humiliating him in front of other students in the small group seminar. As the student states, plaintively:

> *'I fit in, or I fail. And if I try to fight back and preserve myself, well, you're my teacher, you can tear me to pieces in public and mark me down in private. Can't I exist as well?'*

> *(Bradbury, 1975: 148)*

Campus novels are not, of course, particularly reliable guides to what actually goes on in a university but this scene within the novel, even though it represents a caricature, is an illustration of one of the central issues of student academic freedom. Howard Kirk is keen to assert his right to express his Marxist view of the world. In a sense, by doing so he is exercising his freedom as a member of academic faculty. Yet, at the same time, the student feels that his own freedom, to hold a view that contrasts with that of his teacher, is being effectively denied him. As he implores, 'Can't I exist as well?'

Freedom as negative rights

Freedom is one of the most heavily loaded words in the English language. It is loaded in the sense that it is subject to a wide range of definitions and interpretations. There are long lists of types or forms of freedom – religious, economic, political – and more specific examples such as freedom of speech, association and assembly. The word freedom is strongly connected with rights as the latter represent expressions of types of freedom giving individuals, such as citizens in a democratic society, access to certain liberties. The relationship between a government and its citizens has long been understood as a type of unwritten social contract by social and political philosophers. In return for giving elected representatives the power to govern, citizens expect the government to guarantee the protection of certain individual rights. It is when governments fail in this social contract that their legitimacy is called into question.

Most popular expressions of rights (or human rights) in legal documents, such as the US Bill of Rights, tend to reflect an understanding of what are known as *negative rights*. This is the conventional way that rights tend to be thought of: as liberties that individuals are born with and which should not be taken away from them without good reason. Sometimes such rights are referred to as 'inalienable', for example as the right to life or to freedom of speech. A person should not be imprisoned, and have their liberty taken away from them, unless they have committed a serious crime. Here, the role of the government is seen as protecting these pre-existing rights and not, without very good reason, interfering with them or trying to take them away. Negative rights are associated with more politically conservative views where the proper role of government is seen as primarily about the preservation of individual liberties. Negative rights should be enjoyed 'without interference from other persons' (Berlin 1958: 122).

Furthermore, a negative rights perspective is the conventional way in which student academic freedom is understood. The university curriculum can be subject to allegations that its content is biased toward particular theoretical or political perspectives inevitably reflecting the beliefs of the professors who have constructed it. In a university context, this contention flows from the fact that courses are often designed by those that teach and examine. Although in a mass-participation higher education system this form of academic freedom has been eroded in practice, by the development of standardized programs subject to quality assurance systems reflecting the increasing influence of government, university professors still retain considerable autonomy in shaping the nature of the curriculum. Their own research expertise and interests can play an important role in determining course content and themes for exploration. While this may be regarded as a legitimate practice, helping to form a synergy between teaching and research and giving students access to thinking at the cutting edge of the subject, it is indicative of the level of control of the curriculum enjoyed by university professors. This kind of allegation of political bias is commonly leveled at the compulsory school curriculum, but the role of the university professor as a curriculum designer, teacher and examiner is far more pronounced than that of the contemporary schoolteacher.

The curriculum is the conventional focus of attention in discussion about student academic freedom. The question posed is often whether the professoriate, in designing and teaching the university curriculum, and in exercising their own academic freedom, is in some way restricting that of their own students. Choice of course content in respect to either omission or inclusion can be controversial. Many if not most subjects have long running debates concerning the curriculum. High-profile examples include creationism in the biology curriculum or issues of status and classification of musical forms in the music curriculum. Sometimes criticism can focus on the extent to which students are introduced to controversies and debates within the subject itself. In economics, for example, critics have long contended that the university curriculum overly focuses on the role of the subject as a mathematical-model-building science rather than one more broadly focused as a social science, where there might be room for more attention to areas such as economic history, the history of economic thought or development economics (Thornton, 2012).

Attention, though, often focuses on the role that the professoriate might play, deliberately or inadvertently, in influencing student freedom of expression through strident advocacy of particular views. Here, the concern is that professors with charismatic demeanors and strident opinions, such as the fictional Dr. Howard Kirk, can force them on their students and, in the process, retard the extent to which the students are allowed to develop and express their own thinking. This has led to student academic freedom being seen as something that can be *taken away* or *removed* from students by professors as a negative right. It is normally expressed as the freedom from indoctrination or the *right to non-indoctrination* (Moshman, 2009) and is, in a sense, what the young student is pleading for in *The History Man*. The German sociologist Max Weber is closely associated with the view that students should have such a right. He argued that professors should try to stay neutral on political and moral issues rather than using their lectures to promote their own social and political agenda. Conscious of the growing power of politicians and bureaucrats in the German universities during the early years of the twentieth century, Weber saw it as the responsibility of academics to exercise what he called 'self-restraint' (Weber, 1973a: 22).

Weber distinguished between opportunities to profess views in the classroom as opposed to espousing them more widely as a public intellectual. Explaining this view, he argued that there was a difference between proselytizing in the classroom as opposed to public forums or publications where a professor's personal views may be legitimately aired, as might any citizen's (Weber, 1973b: 50). According to Weber, when in a university classroom the professor 'should content himself with the sober execution of a given task: to recognize facts, even those which may be personally uncomfortable, and to distinguish them from his own evaluations' (1973b: 50). At the heart of Weber's concerns was the power imbalance between professors and students and the way that the open expression of the professor's opinion could negatively impact on the academic freedom of the students and weaken their 'taste for sober empirical analysis' (1973b: 53). If professors adopt a stance based on personal bias students might feel intellectually intimidated and hold back from coming forward with their own views. They might, in other words, self-censor.

In contemporary terms, the position advocated by Weber is often described as being 'neutral' or 'balanced'. The professor is adopting, in a sense, a point mid-way between advocacy and apathy (Hanson, 1996). When discussion of controversial topics (e.g. racial politics or gay rights) takes place students may perceive that they will receive lower grades if they disagree with their professor in class (Lusk and Weinberg, 1994). While professors may wish to try to reassure students that such concerns are unjustifiable, perceptions or fears, no matter how unjustified, are harder to alter. Professors are still figures of authority rather than co-learners, despite well-intentioned efforts by some to establish more democratic learning relationships in the classroom. Students depend on professors in order to graduate successfully and this simple but powerful reality means that it takes a very brave – or perhaps, very confident – student to openly disagree with their professor.

In the United States, the debate about student academic freedom has focused almost exclusively on claims that students are being politicized by a left-leaning professoriate trying to radicalize university students by indoctrinating them with a set of 'liberal' values. The events of 9/11 heightened concerns about terrorism and national security on both sides of the Atlantic leading to a reopening of the debate about freedom of speech and extremism on campus. It is claimed by David Horowitz and his US-based campaigning organization, Students for Academic Freedom, that there is a lack of 'balance' in the teaching of controversial subjects and this creates a classroom atmosphere which is intolerant toward students with dissenting views. The effect of this process, according to Horowitz, is that students are prevented from developing their own independent thinking, so raising fears about self-censorship. A 'Student Bill of Rights', produced by Horowitz, focuses exclusively on concerns with respect to indoctrination of students as a violation of their freedoms and the potential impact of related issues, such as unfair assessment, which might affect a student who expresses opinions contrary to those held by their professor (Horowitz, 2002). Similarly, indoctrination is the overriding concern with respect to student academic freedom referred to no less than 30 times in David Moshmann's (2009) book, *Liberty and Learning: Academic Freedom for Teachers and Students.*

The other side of the indoctrination argument is that being 'balanced' unreasonably restricts the academic freedom of the professoriate. As long as professors demonstrate that they evaluate students fairly, they should have the right to express their own views (Nelson, 2010). Despite the concerns raised by Horowitz, the 1915 statement on academic freedom issued by the American Association of University Professors (AAUP) does include a clear instruction to professors that students in their formative years of undergraduate education should be safeguarded from unbalanced approaches:

> The teacher ought also to be especially on his [*sic*] guard against taking unfair advantage of the student's immaturity by indoctrinating him with the teacher's own opinions before the student has had an opportunity fairly to examine other opinions upon the matters in question, and before he has sufficient knowledge and ripeness of judgment to be entitled to form any definitive opinion of his own.
>
> (AAUP, 1915: 298–299)

Horowitz's campaign, though, has led to the AAUP issuing a response entitled Freedom in the Classroom (AAUP, 2007). This statement, published in 2007, affirms that it is a right of teachers to test out their opinion and beliefs on controversial issues in the classroom without regard to the extent to which the views expressed represent opinions based on untested assertions.

There are more practical questions about the extent to which professors can avoid expressing their own beliefs, even if they try not to do so. This is often referred to as 'emotional leakage'. According to this argument, while someone may claim to be committed to a position of neutrality their views will inevitably leak out as a result of their body language, level of enthusiasm or tone of voice, and these signals will be easily detected by observant students. Here, the argument is that those who seek to curtail their freedom of expression will end up conveying their opinions unwittingly. Moreover, there is the attendant risk that they will give less inspiring lectures and compromise their authenticity as a teacher.

The argument about indoctrination illustrates what is sometimes called the 'paradox of freedom' (Gewirth, 1996: 174). The paradox is that more freedom for one party can mean less freedom for another. The exercise of academic freedom by professors can potentially restrict or harm student academic freedom especially where self-censorship takes hold. By the same token, the realization of academic freedom for students might involve restrictions on professorial academic freedom. Examples of this dilemma abound in the wider world and are central to any discussion about rights and freedom. Someone's right or freedom to own an unspoilt beach or a beautiful painting as a strictly private possession effectively removes the freedom of others to experience the aesthetic pleasure of these things. Similarly, one person's exercise of the right to express racial or religious views of an intolerant or critical nature may cause others to feel not just offended but less safe. A number of controversies regarding academic freedom have in recent years focused on whether the desire not to cause offence is unduly curtailing the rights of others (see Chapter 8). In 2013, Universities UK, an umbrella organization for UK institutions, issued a guidance document about external speakers visiting university campuses. The advice to universities appeared to endorse gender segregation where an unsegregated audience might cause offence to the speaker's religious beliefs (Universities UK, 2013). The controversial guidance was later withdrawn following a media storm and criticism from the British prime minister, David Cameron (Hodgson, 2013).

In any free society, a series of freedoms compete for priority. Determining which one should take precedence can be controversial but is a key barometer of the comparative status of particular values within the common culture. The strong and powerful, often occupying privileged positions, tend to be better able to assert their rights or freedoms in comparison with the weaker, poorer and less politically influential members of society. This observation is key to understanding why the freedom of students, as generally the weaker or more vulnerable party in the teaching and learning relationship, may end up coming second to that of the professor or other influential parties, such as sponsors. Hence, the exercise of academic freedom by professors may be understood as causing students correlative 'un-freedom' if their self-expression, access to knowledge or development of their own independent thinking is curtailed in some way. The imbalance of power between professors and students means that professors are inevitably better able to assert their own claims to academic freedom. The unbalanced nature of the literature on academic freedom is very much a symbol of this tension (see Chapter 1).

For this reason the possible effect of professorial academic freedom on the expression of student academic freedom deserves to be taken much more seriously than has previously been the case. Too often there is a tendency for professors to reject the paradoxical nature of freedom by stating that students in their class are always free to express their own opinions. This assertion is normally made sincerely, but with the assumption that students regard their professor's personality and positional power as benign. Student perceptions may be quite different and the risk of self-censorship can never be underestimated. The other weakness of this argument is that having the right to something is not the same as being able to effectively exercise that right. This is where freedom needs to be understood as about having capabilities fostered through positive rights.

Freedom as positive rights

Freedom may be understood quite differently as rights that should be provided or given to someone rather than ones that might already exist and need to be protected from any threat they might be taken away. Factors such as poverty, a lack of education and other forms of economic inequality prevent people from being able to exercise their rights even if they are theoretically, or legally, in possession of them. Freedom is adversely affected by what Sen (1999: 20) has called 'capability deprivation'. For example, if a person is illiterate they will not possess the true capability to exercise their right to vote since they are unable to read and understand the arguments put forward by the various political parties in an electoral campaign. If they do not speak or understand the language of the country in which they are voting, they will be similarly excluded from understanding political debate through the news media. Hence, capability deprivation creates a practical barrier to the exercise of rights. The argument here is that freedom will not just happen by issuing lists of rights endorsed by governments or international bodies. Instead, from a positive rights perspective, there is a need to remove what are sometimes called 'un-freedoms'. These are necessary to the functioning of a decent human society and without them people do not enjoy freedom in a meaningful sense.

Positive rights are ones that are seen as the responsibility of governments and international organizations to confer on individuals. Such rights are associated mainly with a left-leaning set of political ideals where the state plays an active, interventionist role in society to try to reshape it in the interests of equality and social justice. Examples of positive rights include the right to a minimum or 'living' wage, to employment, to a freely accessible or universal health system and to receive an education. The right to receive a fundamental or elementary education has long been recognized under article 26 of the Universal Declaration of Human Rights (UDHR) signed in 1948 (United Nations, 2009). The UDHR further states that higher education should be accessible to all but only on the basis of merit. Hence, only primary education is regarded as an absolute right. Yet it might be argued that such a limited right is not really meaningful in a contemporary society. If an individual is to be able to function in and contribute properly to society they will require more than a basic literacy. They will need access to a more advanced education and to possess a wide range of social and work-related skills. In this sense education may be thought of as an economic and social (or 'positional') good, rather than a right (McCowan, 2010). There is, though, an inherent contradiction in thinking of higher education as a human right and as a positional good at the same time. Higher education can only operate as a positional good, giving advantages to those that successfully participate, if it remains relatively exclusive. If everyone were to benefit from higher education as a right it could no longer be thought of as a positional good in the same way. As McCowan (2013) has argued, higher education can only be thought of as a right in terms of its non-instrumental value. The fact that higher education helps students to obtain better jobs as well as making them into more-educated citizens able to contribute to social and political life are instrumental considerations. Conferring a right 'cannot be conditional on any particular use that it is subsequently put to' (McCowan, 2013: 124). Although rights may be associated with duties they do not carry direct obligations (e.g. to be an active or 'responsible' citizen). This is an important point and one that I believe undermines claims that higher education should develop students as active global citizens (see Chapter 7).

In some contexts access to a university education is seen as a right. In Ecuador access to a free higher education, at least up until undergraduate level, is a constitutional right. In France, students have a right to attend their local university as long as they have passed the baccalaureate (Fernex *et al.*, 2015). Access to university is non-restrictive in large parts of Latin America, for example in Argentina, a country long associated with student academic freedom (see Chapter 3). Yet, the right of access needs to be understood in the context of mass participation systems that are the reality for most higher education students: very large classes, minimal direct contact with professors, and relatively low graduation rates in countries, such as France, where going to university is interpreted as a right. In countries such as Italy and Argentina the freedom to partake of a higher education comes at the price of high non-completion rates. Hence, while the right to higher education may exist, failure to invest in a high-quality public university system results in conditions which run counter to academic achievement for all. A lack of investment can undermine what is meaningful to classify as a positive right. Anyone can enter to run a marathon but only those who have received proper training have much chance of completing one.

Across the globe, we are a long way from seeing access to a higher education as a right. In reality a university education is still largely a privilege rather than something that is conferred universally. Economic, social and cultural barriers make higher education inaccessible to most people. Tuition fees are long established in some international contexts, such as the United States and Japan, but have spread in the last decade across public higher education systems in Europe and Australasia, and also to other parts of the globe with fast developing systems, such East Asia. In the UK (except Scotland), tuition fees, first introduced in 1998, have risen rapidly to become the highest across Europe. This trend, though, is far from universal and a number of southern European countries (e.g. Malta, Cyprus and Greece) and several Scandinavian ones (e.g. Denmark, Finland, Norway and Sweden) have retained free public higher education funding models. In Germany, free tertiary education is a right under the constitution and, after a brief flirtation with tuition fees in both Austria and Germany, these have now been abolished. In the vast majority of countries, however, such a commitment is not regarded as an affordable pledge.

While going to university is not yet generally seen as a positive right in the same way as compulsory schooling, it is fast becoming the norm in many developed nations. Elite systems gave way to universal ones as significant growth in higher education enrolments took place during the 1980s and 1990s. This has produced systems of mass or near universal higher education. In the

United States over 20 million were enrolled in tertiary education by the end of the last decade compared to fewer than 14 million in 2000 (UNESCO, 2012). In Britain, the participation rate in higher education among those under 30 years old had reached almost 50 percent by 2012 (DBIS, 2014). Among developed nations, though, this trend is far from universal. Japan and France, for example, saw little change in higher education enrolments over the last decade. It is now the turn of the developing economies, such as India and China, to experience rapid growth in higher education as previously seen in Western contexts in the 1980s, 1990s and early 2000s. In China, enrolments in tertiary education have increased more than fourfold in less than a decade, rising from 7.3 million in 2000 to over 31 million by 2010 (UNESCO, 2012). In some African countries the growth has been, if anything, even more startling. In Ethiopia, for example, over half a million were enrolled in tertiary education in 2010 compared to just 67,000 a decade earlier (UNESCO, 2012).

Despite this apparently rosy picture, there are still significant socio-economic barriers facing students wishing to enter higher education across the globe. These apply to both developed and developing nations. In low-income countries tertiary-level participation has improved only marginally, from 5 percent in 2000 to 7 percent in 2007. Sub-Saharan Africa has the lowest participation rate in the world at 5 percent. This figure is hardly surprising given that free primary education was only introduced relatively recently in a number of African countries; it started in Kenya in 2003, for example. In Latin America, university enrolment remains at less than half that of high-income countries. Attendance entails significant private costs that average 60 percent of GDP per capita (UNESCO, 2009). This brief review of participation rates around the world illustrates that going to university might be more achievable for the growing middle classes in Western systems and in emerging ones in East Asia and parts of the Middle East, but it is still a long way from being seen as an international right. Sadly, the right to receive a higher education on the basis of merit is largely theoretical. In practice, opportunities tend to relate to the country and class into which someone is born.

It is important, though, to think about rights beyond the concept of access to a higher education. If there is a right to a higher education it can only be meaningful if it further extends to what happens to students both *through* and *within* the educational experience. Mass and open-access higher education systems face the challenge of providing a quality education in terms of good teaching, a well-organized curriculum, suitably challenging but fair assessment regimes, and the provision of appropriate academic and social facilities for students. A university degree should be valued and respected by potential employers. Without these things is the right to a higher education really meaningful? These are rights that might reasonably be expected *through* a higher education. While in France all students passing their baccalaureate may enjoy the right to gain *access* to a public university, arguably those who win places through competitive examinations to enter the elite Grandes Écoles ultimately enjoy superior career and further academic opportunities *through* their higher education. There are further rights *within* a higher education that relate to the manner in which students are treated while they are studying at university. This is avowedly the main focus of this book.

The right of access to education, the right to a quality education and the right to respect within the learning community are the three integrative components proposed in a UNICEF/UNESCO report (UNICEF/UNESCO, 2007). They mirror the conceptual distinctions between the right *to* education, rights *through* education and rights *within* education identified by a number of authors as a suitable overarching heuristic for understanding educational rights (e.g. McCowan, 2013). While the UNICEF/UNESCO report relates to compulsory schooling, the applicability of this rights framework to a higher education context are obvious. Considerable attention has tended to focus on the right *to* education as an issue of social justice and to rights *through* education, particularly from an employability perspective. This has been used to justify the introduction or lifting of university tuition fees by governments around the world. Less attention, I would contend, has focused on rights *within* education that relate directly to how students are treated by universities as learners while they are studying.

The importance of the perspective offered by positive rights is that it is not meaningful to talk about rights if they are purely theoretical or do not have any real, practical import. A person needs to be capable of exercising their rights not merely being in possession of them. This brings us back to the capability approach advocated by Sen (1999) and Nussbaum (2003). Adopting a positive right and capabilities approach, Garnett (2009: 442) has argued that university students should enjoy basic freedoms to have their work fairly evaluated, to be allowed to question the premises of the discipline they are studying, to explore a curriculum that is representative of competing disciplinary perspectives, and to 'learn the art of thinking critically within their discipline'. The second and third of these freedoms reflect the debate about student academic freedom in the US focused on concerns about potential bias within the curriculum. It offers an application of a capabilities approach within the context of fears about indoctrination. Even though this is an important perspective on student academic freedom there are further dimensions that deserve attention linked to student performativity (see Chapters 5–7).

Students need to be given the capability to be able to become independent learners, and to develop their knowledge and skills in order that they can make their own decisions and choices about what to study and, ultimately, what to believe in. These are positive rights that need to be developed *within* (higher) education. This has to happen within higher education as they are not simply conferred or developed by dint of gaining access *to* higher education or in the advantages derived socially and materially *through* taking a university course. In order to become independent thinkers students need an environment that fosters their choices as adults.

Whose academic freedom?

There is a substantial literature on freedom and different ways of interpreting this loaded term. Much the same might be said for the phrase 'academic freedom' which itself is the subject of considerable academic analysis. In addition to numerous books and scholarly articles, there are policy statements by universities and professional associations, such as the AAUP, and by campaigning organizations, such as Scholars at Risk, Academics for Academic Freedom (AFAF) and the Council for Academic Freedom and Academic Standards (CAFAS). These various groups are dedicated to keeping issues connected with academic freedom at the forefront of news and political debate.

Concerns with respect to freedom of expression of academic faculty remain central to the functioning of academic life. But what does academic freedom mean? The answer to this apparently simple question is not straightforward. Academic freedom is a complex and contested concept. At its heart it implies the protection of the right of scholars to teach and enquire without fear of losing their jobs or to be otherwise intimidated. Its historical antecedents can be traced back to the medieval European universities of the eleventh and twelfth centuries (Karran, 2009). There are different interpretations of, and justifications for, academic freedom. In the German tradition, Wilhelm von Humboldt's functional view was that permitting scholars the freedom or independence to enquire benefited government as they were more likely to produce research which would make a difference to society (Coleman, 1977). How far this freedom should extend remains a matter of some controversy. Some argue that academic freedom should be confined to disciplinary expertise, while others, supporting the concept of 'extramural freedom' (Metzger, 1987: 1265), consider that scholars should be allowed to engage more broadly on matters of public policy, and as political activists, beyond the narrow confines of their disciplinary backgrounds (AAUP, 1915).

Yet there is something important that is missing here. In all of the discussion and debate about academic freedom there is rarely any mention of students. What rights, if any, do they have with respect to academic freedom? In the preceding paragraph I was careful to refer to 'scholars' but few would read this passage and be in doubt that it referred exclusively to academic faculty. They would simply assume it. Comparatively little has been written or said about the freedom of students – in notable contrast with the attention afforded to those that teach them. As others have noted, the role of the student in relation to academic freedom has been long neglected (Bissell, 1969). Implicitly, and sometimes explicitly, those who write about academic freedom assign its privileges to faculty rather than students. Ellen Schrecker is not untypical of this tendency when she writes:

> In its traditional form, *academic freedom belongs above all to the faculty*. It is the system of procedures and protections that allows learning and scholarship

to take place on the nation's campuses. It makes it possible for members of the academic profession to speak freely inside and outside their classrooms and to publish the results of their research without fear that they will be dismissed or otherwise punished by the institutions that employ them.

(Schrecker, 2010: 4–5; my italics)

This is the conventional way we tend to think about academic freedom; namely that the right to speak freely is a protection that applies to the academic profession. In Schrecker's words 'academic freedom belongs *above all* to the faculty' (my italics). Students, it seems, are not equal members of the academic community, if indeed they are members of it at all. Much of the literature about academic freedom reinforces this one-dimensional understanding of the concept, making only fleeting reference to students or sometimes overlooking their importance altogether. Conrad Russell's book *Academic Freedom* (1993) is an example of this apparent myopia, containing absolutely no reference to students.

Student academic freedom is a neglected concept for a number of other reasons. The right of academics to academic freedom is safeguarded by legal statute in a number of countries including the UK. The tendency to exclude students from legal expressions about entitlement to academic freedom overlooks the importance of developing learners with the capacity to function as informed and critical members of civic society, something that might be thought of as a positive right. Although students are formally members of a community of scholars, they essentially occupy a position of dependence in that they are subject to the authority of their teachers and institutions in respect to grading and the certification of their achievement through the award of degrees (Monypenny, 1963). Ultimately, the real power rests with professors and their institutions, and with this comes the authority to determine the extent to which they treat students as real members of the academic community when it comes to the privileges of academic freedom.

As I will suggest later in the book, another of the barriers to thinking of students as scholars is that we increasingly defer to the market analogy (see Chapters 4 and 8). As a result of this students are labeled as customers, rather than members of the academic community. Perversely this means that they have a reduced status as members of the academic community. The hierarchical nature of academic life further means that the student is cast in the role of a novice. Although rarely stated explicitly in a contemporary context, an implicit, but patronizing, assumption is that students, as novices or scholars in training, do not possess the knowledge necessary to make sufficiently informed judgments (Horn, 1999). Their knowledge base is developing compared to that of the professors who teach them. The view here is that academic faculty develop and disseminate new knowledge, not students (Schrecker, 2010); they are the ones developing and testing claims to new knowledge. Hence, if professors, rather than students, are the ones more likely to be breaking new ground intellectually then, so the argument goes, they are the ones that need a greater measure of protection in expressing their views. It follows that students, as apprentices or novice members of the academic community, require less protection as they are not risking their necks in putting forward a controversial new theory or contradicting received wisdom. Furthermore, professors have jobs and careers at universities that might be threatened in some way if they are not protected. Students are learning to be academics in some respects and, as such, it is only when they become fully fledged members of the academic profession that they deserve the protection afforded by academic freedom. A further argument is that students, especially undergraduates, are in a sense just 'passing through' higher education institutions for a few years, unlike members of academic faculty who spend their careers at the university. From this perspective, students are not really committed to scholarship or to the university as an institution on a long-term basis. This view has been further bolstered in recent years by the way that students have been transformed into 'customers'. This has had the perverse effect of diminishing rather than enhancing their rights. It means that they are regarded as participants in an economic transaction rather than members of an academic community committed to their personal development as scholars, professionals and citizens. These arguments adopt a patronizing attitude toward students within the educational process and imply that their relationship is a market-based, transactional one. As I will argue in Chapter 8, casting students as 'customers' erodes rather than enhances their rights. They might be better able and more expected to complain and demand value for money in a market-based system but this results in a perception that students are organizational outsiders rather than budding intellectuals and autonomous adults who deserve the freedom to learn.

It might further be argued that, while academic freedom is largely self-referential, this is essential in order to protect the freedom of others. Put another way, although the protection tends to apply principally to academics rather than students, the role of the professoriate is to use their freedom to protect their students' freedom. It is essential that academics use their academic freedom to protect the rights of others to express their own beliefs, including their own students. This makes the professor the guardian of the student's academic freedom. The argument here is that it is only when academic faculty are free that they will be in a position to expose students to the range of ideas and arguments that will, in turn, help them to find their own voice and develop fully as learners. While this may be true, interpreting student academic freedom in this way treats it as little more than a by-product of the freedom of the academic profession, a view that might, at best, be described as condescending. It presumes that members of the academic profession will take full advantage of the privileges of academic freedom to assert this right and to use it to protect their own students. While the 1915 AAUP statement on academic freedom made reference to student academic freedom, the focus of the report was the academic freedom of the teacher (AAUP, 1915). Where students were mentioned in the statement it is by reference to how their freedom is inhibited or facilitated by that of the teacher.

These self-referential interpretations of academic freedom are insufficient. They overlook the important role of a higher education in encouraging students, not just academic faculty, to adopt a critical approach to knowledge claims (Barnett, 1990). Students need to be able to evaluate claims to knowledge without inhibition or restriction. Postgraduate students are very often engaged in completing pieces of independent research which require the protection of academic freedom. Doctoral students need to produce work that makes a new contribution to knowledge in order to graduate. Surely to achieve this high ambition they need and deserve academic freedom in challenging existing under-standings and interpretations? The received wisdom students may choose to challenge will invariably be based on the research and publications of academics. If they are not permitted to challenge it, how can new knowledge be created?

Conclusion

Student academic freedom needs to be understood as implying both negative and positive rights. Self-censorship is a genuine threat to student academic freedom from a negative rights perspective but should not constitute the dominant or only way in which this concept is understood. There is a need to move beyond this lim-ited interpretation to one that includes positive rights. If students are to be able to develop their own capabilities as independent learners and thinkers, they need to be provided with the choices, opportunities, encouragement and conducive environ-ment in which to do so. Restrictions in the way in which students learn at university need to be kept to a minimum to allow different forms of engagement with knowl-edge in many ways – via discussion, interaction, writing, reading, reflection and listening. Coercing students to learn in particular ways, such as via discussion and interaction, needs to be avoided, along with labeling some as in any way superior to others because they are 'active' as opposed to 'passive' (see Chapter 4).

Both academic faculty and students are, in essence, learners or scholars enquir-ing together. They are members of the same university community. Students may be less knowledgeable than professors, but they require the same protections in order to be allowed access to the common project of academic life: testing out claims to truth in both theory and practice contexts. It follows that the privileges of academic freedom ought to apply to students as well as professors. While stu-dents may only be novice scholars, they are not the only ones learning. Academic faculty are engaged in the same process too – a lifelong pursuit of greater under-standing in the spirit of curiosity allied to personal and ideological values. The word 'inclusive' has become a mantra in higher education in relation to adopting a more welcoming attitude to minorities or disadvantaged groups. Universities are full of policies seeking to promote equal opportunities. Yet, despite the rhetoric of inclusivity in the modern university, students are rarely treated as members of the academic family and accorded equality in terms of protection of their academic freedom. There is a need to expand the way in which this concept is understood in the university beyond the freedom of the professoriate.

Chapter 3

A paradox

How Ted Turner got sent down

In 1960, a young undergraduate student called Ted Turner was expelled from Brown University. The reason for his expulsion was that he was caught with a girl in his room at the university's residential hall. A few years later Turner took over his father's ailing advertising business. He managed to turn the business around and later went on to become one of the world's richest and most successful media tycoons. Most famously he founded Cable News Network (CNN), the first 24-hour cable news service. His celebrity status has owed much to the fact that one of his three marriages was to Jane Fonda, a prominent American movie star. As a multi-billionaire who is estimated to be the largest private landowner in the US, Turner has become a significant philanthropist giving millions of dollars to the United Nations.

Unsurprisingly, after expelling Turner back in 1960, his former university later became keen to rebuild bridges with its ex-student. Brown University awarded Turner a number of honorary degrees insisting that as someone who had attended the institution he was really an alumnus even though he did not graduate. Brown University benefited hugely from this about face with Turner becoming one of its largest ever donors. Keen to play down the expulsion incident 40 years earlier Lisa Raiola, the Vice President for Alumni Relations, remarked in 2004 that 'He wasn't doing anything that would be considered serious by our standards today' (Grin, 2004).

The story of Ted Turner's expulsion from Brown University is symbolic of an almost forgotten era of student life in Western higher education. Turner had committed what was considered a serious moral indiscretion by the standards of 1960. Yet, as the Brown vice president suggested in 2004, freedom in respect to romantic and sexual relationships between consenting adults had become little more than a personal lifestyle choice by the turn of the century rather than a basis for expelling a student. While restrictions on personal lifestyle choices may still exist in some higher education systems, especially in parts of East Asia and the Middle East, such restrictions are now rare in the West. Yet, the case of Ted Turner shows just how recently such attitudes have changed.

The roots of strict disciplinary policies affecting a student's choice of activities, liaisons and lifestyle choices may be traced back to the fifteenth century (Cardozier, 1968). Prior to this, considerable power lay in the hands of the students rather than the professors who were reliant on negotiating fees, as at Bologna, rather than receiving a steady income. Students enjoyed real power in university governance and an extraordinary range of liberties, including freedom from taxation, military service or trial in civil courts (Norton, 1909). The idea of students and professors in co-governance implied that both enjoyed equality of status (de Figueiredo-Cowen, 2002). From the fifteenth century a gradual shift of power to university authorities occurred as more professors gained endowed positions, student rectors were replaced and city authorities made greater financial contributions to university funds (Cardozier, 1968).

Universities were in the main small residential communities that had been modeled on medieval Catholic monasteries. Many early British, and later American, colleges were based on a quadrangle, an inward-facing courtyard such as may be found in medieval monasteries. The monastic roots of this architectural design were a symbol of both scholarly contemplation and a self-sacrificing morality. The role of these ancient universities in preparing students to enter the clergy meant that they were as much, if not more, concerned with the social and moral development of students as with their intellectual advancement. The universities of Oxford and Cambridge in England and the early institutions in the United States such as William and Mary, Harvard, Yale, and Brown, where Ted Turner studied, placed considerable emphasis on what were regarded as correct standards of moral behavior (Gallagher and Demos, 1983). Strict disciplinary rules came to govern the lives of students. Masters of these residential establishments were in control and severely punished those who did not abide by the rules. Restrictions applied to who might visit and when, along with the time when students could leave and return to halls of residence.

Students would be 'rusticated' (i.e. punished) for a period of time for committing a disciplinary offence. Ultimately, a student could be 'sent down' or expelled from university for persistent misbehavior or stepping out of line in a significant way. The close ties between universities and the church, in European as well as South and North American contexts, meant that institutions came to regard the social and moral conduct of students as its legitimate business. The religious and familial connection of the universities came to be symbolized by the residential college. This provided a cloistered, and quasi-monastic retreat from the world and, with it, a prevailing atmosphere of moral austerity (Jackson, 1991).

The power of the church in university affairs was not a uniquely English tradition. It existed in several other contexts including the United States where, from the seventeenth through to the nineteenth century, institutions were established with similar objectives to those in England, to produce ministers to serve the established church and to produce Christian gentlemen (McCormick and Meiners, 1988). The residential character of universities was a key part of fulfilling such goals and the college system ensured that the behavior and moral development of individual students could be closely monitored and controlled. The lasting importance of the residential college was such that it was still being identified as part of the distinctive tradition of British higher education as late as the early 1970s (Halsey and Trow, 1971).

A history of violence between town and gown dating back to medieval times lay behind some of the more anachronistic regulations. At Oxford, a statute dating from the seventeenth century barred students from visiting townspeople in their homes, taking part in potentially dangerous games, carrying weapons or hanging around on the streets (Batson, 2008). A number of students charged with being homosexual were expelled from Harvard during the 1920s, demonstrating that draconian policies affecting the private lives of students were just as common in US universities with roots in the late eighteenth century. Severe disciplinary regimes affecting university students were still largely in place during the early part of the twentieth century, although they began to come under increasing pressure as social rules relaxed following the end of the First World War. By then women and religious minorities had started to gain access to higher education. Yet, even in the 1920s women students at Oxford were not permitted to be alone with a man, unless he was a brother, either on or off college grounds. Until 1923 women students at Oxford were not even permitted to talk with their male counterparts at lectures. They, in turn, were forbidden to enter a female's room under any circumstances (Batson, 2008). Restrictions concerning drinking, dancing and mixed parties affected both male and female students.

The changing campus

The restrictions on the way in which students conducted their private lives may look like ancient history but were, in reality, still in place in the middle part of the last century. They symbolize an age when relationships between the sexes were considered a legitimate matter for moral and religious censorship. The standards of social and moral behavior which were expected of students even as recently as the 1960s now appear to have little relevance in Western higher education today but, as Ted Turner's case illustrates, it is only in comparatively recent times that attitudes to rules governing the conduct of a student's private life have shifted.

We now live in an age of mass participation in higher education, an international trend that is a feature of nearly all developed economies. Aside from changing social attitudes, mass participation in higher education has altered the nature of university life in other ways. It is no longer the exclusive preserve of a tiny elite of the young and privileged living in cloistered residential surroundings. Modern-day higher education is open to all on the basis of merit and the contemporary student is far more likely to be mature, in employment, studying part-time and living off campus. The decline of the residential model of the university is a significant change. This has come about as more and more students live at home and attend a local institution to defray the costs of tuition in an increasingly market-driven system. The fact that students are less likely to be living on the campus of the university means that their private lives are largely beyond the reach of higher education institutions. Proscribing certain types of behavior and relationships is highly impractical when students live off campus and may spend much of their time doing things other than simply being a 'student', such as working full- or part-time. Trying to govern a student's private life is not only out of tune with contemporary social values; it is further, perhaps more significantly, an entirely impractical proposition given the myriad ways in which students engage in university learning – at work, part-time and increasingly online or through mobile devices.

Most university students in the Western world now enjoy personal freedom to conduct their private lives as they choose. There may, of course, be other checks on how students live their private lives depending on their familial, cultural and religious background, but as far as universities are concerned this is no longer any of their business. While students are still subject to rules and regulations in respect to their behavior on the physical or virtual campus, these focus mainly on issues of safety and illegal activity such as the possession and use of illicit drugs or the use of abusive or offensive language in online forums. Their rights – whether on the basis of their race, religion, gender or sexual orientation – are safeguarded by equal opportunities, anti-discrimination and Lesbian, Gay, Bisexual and Transgender (LGBT) officers. Disabled students, whatever the nature of their impairments, must be supported and given equal access to university facilities. Anyone wishing to involve students in research must ensure their informed consent is obtained and guarantee their anonymity as part of ethical approval procedures.

The decline of the concept of the personal or moral tutor is a reflection of changing social mores about the private lives of students. A personal tutor with a responsibility for the welfare and moral guidance of young students was once a distinctive feature of English higher education, mimicking the role played by so-called moral tutors at Oxford and Cambridge universities. Today, most English universities still formally retain a system of personal tutors but their contemporary role is very different to the moral tutor of old. They are now primarily regarded as a means of supporting students in adapting to life at university and in offering a friendly and non-judgmental ear if the student encounters any personal problems. In explaining their role, most universities are at pains to point out that they do not seek to pry into a student's private life. Nowadays personal tutors act more as referral agents for other specialist support officers who can offer help on social, psychological and practical problems such as debt-management, housing or counselling for depression and other mental health services. Universities now regard the role of the personal tutor pragmatically as helping to stem the drop-out or 'attrition' rate, something that will directly affect the university's revenue stream. Providing student support contributes positively to the bottom line rather than offering a moral correction service.

From child to adult

The 1960s marked a significant change in the relationship between students and universities in North America and Europe, in particular. Higher education institutions had always acted *in loco parentis*, as replacement parents, taking it upon themselves to discipline or punish students under their care. This paternalism, or moral guardianship, was eroded by a series of legal decisions in the US, most notably *Dixon v. Alabama State Board of Education* in 1961, when a group of Black students successfully challenged their expulsion from college for protesting against racial segregation policies. The court ruled that the constitutional rights of the students to due process had been violated and that the institution could not simply rely on *in loco parentis* as a defence.

The lowering of the age of majority in 1970 in the UK, and shortly after in most US states, meant that university students were now legally adults at age 18, at the beginning of their higher education, rather than 21 when, for most, their studies were coming to an end. Internationally, 18 years of age has become the norm, although the age of majority in a number of Canadian provinces and some US states remains at 19, while in Japan and Taiwan it is 20, and in parts of Africa, the Middle East and Singapore it is still 21. The age of adulthood is complex and ambiguous with countries applying a series of different ages to signify adulthood in the context of a range of responsibilities and actions. In Taiwan, for example, while the age of majority is 20, responsibility for criminal acts is assumed at the earlier age of 18. Matters are complicated further by the fact that in some higher education systems, such as Hong Kong, students go to university at 17 rather than 18 years of age. While acknowledging this complexity, in most national systems students are legally recognized as having attained adulthood when they enter university, or very shortly after. Therefore, in this book, I will refer to university students as adults and argue that they should be treated as such. This point is critical to my argument that, in thinking about the freedoms of students, they need to be treated in the same manner as an adult person.

There is a difference, though, between the extent to which university students are legally acknowledged as adults and the extent to which they are treated as such. More paternalistic attitudes toward students exist in some cultural contexts, particularly in East Asia, where it is commonplace for university presidents to refer to students as 'my children'. Here, Confucian philosophy plays a role in the attitudes of university presidents, academics and students. According to Confucius, 'Even if someone is your teacher for only a day, you should regard him like your father for the rest of your life' (Watson, 1969: 100). The importance of filial piety within Chinese families and wider society helps to explain the patriarchal culture of East Asian university life. This plays out in a number of practical ways both in the teaching and learning environment, where class registers are commonplace, and in social life on campus. Alcohol is less likely to be found on campus as part of the services offered by students' unions in developing contexts in East Asia for cultural reasons. While (most) students may be legally of age to drink alcohol, it is rare to find bars open to them on a Hong Kong university campus or in other East Asian universities.

University policy statements now emphasize their duty of care toward students not as minors who need moral guidance but as users of a facility, like customers or employees, who deserve a safe and secure environment. Some have argued that *in loco parentis* appears to have been reinvented for a more litigious age in which students and their parents are exercising increasing power and influence as customers and consumers of educational services.

> Students began to expect their colleges to get them jobs, to provide them with tuition assistance and establish their careers. Further, the students demanded protections – protections against criminal attack, against harm inflicted by others, and against injuries sustained often due to their own care-lessness. In short, students began to ask colleges to take care of them much like their parents did.
>
> (Szablewicz and Gibbs, 1987: 453)

Parents may well be the ones acting in an assertive manner in holding institutions to account for the safety and security of their offspring where, for instance, students have been seriously injured or died on campus as a result of the use of illegal drugs or have committed suicide. Such incidents would have formerly been seen as indicative of the students' defective moral character. Now such incidents are defined in terms of failure on the part of the institution in exercising its duty of care toward its students. This new interpretation has led some institutions, such as the University of Alberta in Canada, to ban the consumption of alcohol in common areas within residential halls as it is seen as a potential health and safety risk. It is another example of how university authorities, increasingly concerned about the possibility of litigation and reputational damage, have been forced to exercise a stronger duty of care toward their student population in respect to their physical and mental well-being. It is a further reason why there has been an expansion in student support services in recent years as universities seek to demonstrate that they are meeting their obligations.

In most respects, the personal freedom enjoyed by university students today has never been so great. Their private lives are now respected as such and are no longer seen as the legitimate object of 'moral' censorship by universities. The lowering of the age of majority to 18, signifying legal recognition of the attainment of adult-hood, occurred in large parts of the world during the 1960s and 1970s. This has played a significant part in bringing about this change of attitude together with a shift to what is sometimes pejoratively labeled the 'permissive society', a phrase associated with the relaxation of social norms, particularly in respect to sexual freedom. It was only as recently as the 1970s and 1980s that 'students in general were no longer seen, at least not to the same extent, as children over whom some moral oversight must perforce be exercised, and there was no longer the same felt urgency to keep the sexes apart' (Tight, 2011: 110). While assumptions regarding the integral nature of university accommodation to a higher education and its actual provision reached its high point in the 1960s and 1970s, it was also the beginning of important changes. Subsequently, the residential model of university education has fallen into decline for both economic and social reasons. Some of the wider social benefits that students derived from living on campus may have been lost but they are now far freer to live as they choose.

Political freedom

Political freedom is something that many students studying in a Western context take for granted. Enjoying the right to elect their political leaders and to criticize and ultimately unseat them is a given in democratic contexts. By political freedom I am referring to the extent to which students are able to play a role in political debate and determine who governs them as well as participate in university decision-making at a local level as members of the academic community (see Table 3.1). I would not limit it, as others have, to involvement in university administration to the exclusion of wider participation in national political debate and activity (Klemenčič, 2012). As I will argue, this is a limitation that largely domesticates and de-politicizes the role of students.

Political freedom is a right which has been hard won and students, particularly in some developing higher education systems, have played and continue to play important roles in campaigning to secure it on behalf of the wider population at a national level. This is no better exemplified than in parts of East Asia where students from higher education institutions based in Hong Kong, Taiwan and South Korea have all taken to the streets in recent years and risked life and limb in leading democratic movements (Macfarlane, 2016; Shin *et al.*, 2014). In other contexts, for example South Africa, the focus of student protest can be on issues connected with the continuing impact of historic legacies of inequality

Table 3.1 Three types of student freedom

Personal freedom	The freedom to live in the way one chooses, free from interference; also sometimes known as individual freedom. Students should be allowed to make their own lifestyle choices related to moral conduct, sexual behavior and identity, including relationships and living arrangements.
Political freedom	The freedom of citizens to determine who governs them and to be free to evaluate and criticize their rulers. Students should play a significant role in university governance and decision-making processes and have political freedom of expression.
Freedom to learn	The freedom to decide what, when and where to study. Students should be treated with respect as autonomous adults with the right to make choices about their study program that meet their personal needs and objectives.

and injustice, such as the campaign involving both academic faculty and students asking for the removal of a statue of Cecil Rhodes at The University of Cape Town in 2015 (Hall, 2015). The 'Rhodes Must Fall' campaign is not just concerned with removing a statue of a man considered an icon of colonialism and racism but as part of a process of challenging the pace of change within higher education and wider society in post-apartheid South Africa. This campaign has gone international and Oxford University's Oriel College has been challenged to remove a plaque commemorating Cecil Rhodes from one of its buildings (Matthews, 2015).

The idea of students being involved in the governance of the university has a long history in the Latin American tradition and can be traced back to the thirteenth-century medieval institutions at Bologna and Salamanca (Einaudi, 1963; de Figueiredo-Cowen, 2002). Events at the university of Córdoba in Argentina in 1918 rekindled the spirit of this medieval tradition when students made a series of demands for university reform. These included reducing the influence of the Catholic Church and student participation in electing university professors. The students won a series of concessions giving them powers to elect representatives to the university administration, increasing their policy influence, and allowing them optional class attendance and more flexible examination arrangements. The Córdoba reforms spread to a large number of universities in Argentina and elsewhere in Latin America, including Chile, Peru and Uruguay. Hence, although popular awareness of students in university politics tends to be most closely associated with student movements in the US, France and the UK during the 1960s, its real roots lie in Latin America and considerably pre-date the so-called 'swinging sixties'.

The Córdoba reforms were a significant period in Latin American university life and much of the spirit of this time was rekindled in the 1960s and early 1970s when student protests once more came to the fore. These were times of significant social change with the decline of deference for the authority of the post-war order. Students around the world, notably in the US, Canada, France, Germany, Mexico and the UK, demonstrated their support for the civil rights movement and women's rights, and their opposition to nuclear weapons. In the US, students supported the rights of African-Americans and protested against the Vietnam War. These were the headline issues of the day and a focus for student politics and protest. Yet, the student radicalism of the 1960s and 1970s in high-profile campaigns such as those opposing apartheid in South Africa or the Vietnam War have not converted into increased influence in the running of their own institutions in the same way in which the Córdoba reforms were principally intended. The shift from collegial to managerial control of the university has undermined the extent to which both academic faculty and students have any real say in the governance of their institutions. This is mainly because university presidents and vice chancellors are under increasing pressure of accountability to external rather than internal constituencies (Waugh, 2003). Governance structures have decreased the number of those participating internally and, instead, most university boards now have a larger proportion of external members (Rochford, 2014). This means that both the professoriate and the student population are seen as employees and customers rather than as a community of organizational members with a central role in the governance structure.

While student representation in decision-making processes used to be considered a key issue in debate about the democratization of universities in the late 1960s and 1970s, the shift to a more managerial culture has resulted in students being largely excluded from discussion except as clients (Luescher-Mamashela, 2010). This may be illustrated by reference to parts of East Asia where democracy has only recently been established. Student activism contributed to the democratic reform process in South Korea during the late 1980s but has since been replaced by 'individualist and pragmatist values spread throughout university communities, which shifted students' interest to personal issues including school or leisure, and away from socio-political issues' (Shin et al., 2014: 452). Such changes echo the way in which the role of students has transitioned in Western contexts over the last 30 years from that of a member of the academic community at the heart of university governance to a client or customer of the university (Rochford, 2008).

In a Western context, students enjoy an unprecedented level of personal freedom and live in liberal democracies where political freedom is part of the fabric of civil society. Yet, in these contexts, there is a domestication of the political dimension of student freedom taking place as the forces of marketization and privatization play a steadily more influential role in university affairs and the strategic decision-making of institutions. This is the key paradox I wish to draw attention to in the final part of this chapter.

Domestication and de-politicization

Institutions now define student engagement in university governance in ways that reflect the increasing marketization and commodification of higher education. Students are encouraged to undertake representative activities on behalf of the student body as a means of enhancing their work-related skills in order to differentiate themselves from their peers in a crowded jobs market. Academics, administrators and student union officers define the role of a student representative in terms of institutional and personal objectives, such as graduate employability skills and the enhancement of CVs for the jobs market (Carey, 2013). Being a 'rep' entails practicing skills such as participating in events and networking while gaining recognition and kudos for taking on a representative role in the process (Little et al., 2009). Within these narrow confines becoming a student representative is now being defined principally as a form of CV-building or what has been termed 'self-commodification' (Edmond and Berry, 2014: 13), a process of converting the self into a product suitable for the knowledge-based economy (Roderick, 2010). This may sometimes be referred to as personal branding.

What is significant is that defining student engagement as a form of self-commodification has become the dominant discourse not just of the university's management and careers services but of student unions too. The guidance produced by student unions on becoming a student or course representative now mainly emphasizes how such a role produces personal benefits related to skills-development, contributing, in a UK context, to a so-called Higher Education Achievement Report (HEAR). This is an electronic document detailing a student's academic and other non-academic achievements at university, such as 'extra-curricular activities, prizes and employability awards, voluntary work and offices held in student union clubs and societies that have been verified by the institution' (HEAR, 2015). It specifically seeks to incorporate information about student union activities within a document intended to capture a students' employability skills. The HEAR, which was first introduced into UK higher education in 2008, has now been adopted by 90 UK universities (HEAR, 2015). Explanations of the benefits of acting as a student representative produced by student unions now reflect this domestication of the role of 'student rep' within the HEAR:

> becoming a Rep is an experience that gives you many skills which you can add to your CV.
>
> (Sussex University Student Union)

> Being an officer also gives you valuable and varied experience that will look great on your CV and help when applying for jobs in the future.
>
> (University College London Student Union)

> More and more employers are recognising the benefits of candidates who have proven that they'll go that extra mile. This is a chance to improve your CV, get invaluable free training and have some fun!
>
> (Manchester University Student Union)

> For most UCL undergraduates, your volunteering can now be included upon the HEAR (Higher Education Achievement Report). The HEAR contains your academic record, but also includes extra-curricular activities such as volunteering.
>
> (University College London Student Union)

These comments cited in Edmond and Berry (2014: 12) are illustrative of the way in which what is now popularly referred to as the 'student voice' is being domesticated in the service of what has been described as a 'de-politicised form of student activism and the adoption of a consumerist student political discourse' (Luescher-Mamashela, 2010: 259). De-politicization of student politics has occurred under pressure from a more pragmatic set of concerns centering on skills development and employment prospects.

Defining students as so-called stakeholders in the educational process and seeking to involve them in decision-making processes may appear respectful and democratic. Yet, it shifts the role of the student representative from an agent of the student body to a servant of the wider corporate interests of the institution. Universities are keen to increase student participation in decision-making processes as part of this agenda even though one study estimated that fewer than 20 percent of student representatives are active (Carey, 2013). This is, perhaps, a reflection of the fact that it is the institution and not the students who are determining the basis of their engagement as part of the quality assurance infrastructure of the university. In Carey's (2013: 1297) study of student representation the 'general concern' of academics, administrators and students was that 'the system played to the institution's agenda and not the students'. When the university is controlling the agenda for engagement there is little opportunity for a more radical version of the student voice to emerge.

There are other ways in which universities like to bring students 'into the tent' (Rochford, 2014: 485). They encourage them to direct their energies toward institutionally sanctioned and sanctified causes such as global citizenship or campaigning for the ending of world poverty (see Chapter 7). While it might seem perverse to question the university's sincerity in promoting such worthy causes, they are politically correct or 'safe' ones to adopt. They have become mainstream and conventional in political discourse and are relatively non-contentious aspirations that relate to global rather than potentially more controversial and sensitive local, regional or national issues such as the privatization of the university or high levels of student tuition fees and debt. Universities issuing commitments to 'safe' global causes have much in common with large business organizations for whom corporate social responsibility is now integral to wider strategic objectives and market positioning. Regardless of the motive though, by adopting such causes, and often incorporating such issues within the curriculum in some manner, the university is straying into territory previously occupied by the student body. By formalizing what has conventionally been reactive and informal in response to events, it subtly takes ownership of this domain of activity and defines an agenda that might have formerly been determined by the student body.

Despite this process of domestication there are still those within the student body prepared to protest at the growing marketization of higher education. This has become, in Western contexts where the market-based model of higher education has come to the fore, the cause célèbre of the age. In Germany a number of federal states introduced tuition fees in 2006 and 2007. The opposition movement took the form of mass student protests, fee strikes and student occupations and attracted considerable public support, something largely absent from the campaign against the tripling of tuition fees in England in 2010. The weight of student and public opposition persuaded the federal German states to abandon tuition fees. In Canada, another federal system of higher education, mass student protests against the raising of tuition fees in Quebec took place in 2012. Students opposed the proposed increase of average annual fees from C$2,168 to C$3,793. The government had planned to phase in this fee hike over a six-year period but their proposal was met by street protests, picketing and student occupations. While the proposed increase was modest, certainly compared with tuition fees in US or UK terms, it was abandoned later in 2012 following the election of a new minority government in Quebec. Events in Germany and Quebec show that marketization is not an inevitable process and that student activism, where it attracts significant public support, can be effective.

Student opposition to tuition fee increases have been less successful in the UK. Sources of frustration and objects of protest amongst students at UK universities such as Birmingham, Edinburgh, Sheffield, University College London and Warwick include the privatization of student debt, the pay of senior university managers and the outsourcing of campus services (Evans, 2013). The subject of these protests is sometimes represented as self-regarding in focusing on issues affecting the economic well-being of students. However, such a characterization fails to capture wider political concerns centering on the marketization and privatization of the university.

In 2013, student protests took place at both Birmingham and Sussex universities against plans by university management to outsource campus services to private companies. These protests indicate the way in which university authorities now define the limits of student engagement. In December 2013, five students were suspended from the University of Sussex for allegedly occupying a building in protest at the university's plans to outsource campus services affecting over 230 support jobs, such as catering, cleaning, portering services and security. This was seen by protesters as an attempt to privatize the university and worsen the employment conditions of support staff whose jobs were due to be subcontracted to a private service provider. Fears were raised that many faced the prospect of either losing their jobs or being re-employed on inferior contracts. The protesters argued that outsourcing such services would result in profits being paid to shareholders of private companies rather than being reinvested into improving campus facilities. The university management responded to the demonstrations by strengthening the presence of private security and suspending five student protesters who they accused of leading serious disruption on campus resulting in intimidating behavior, theft and violence. The university's management was, however, later forced to retract the suspensions and the allegations against the so-called 'Sussex 5' and also pay compensation, following the decision of an independent ombudsman that the suspensions were unreasonable. The decision followed a social media campaign with the students winning the support of a number of celebrities who joined in the condemnation of the university's actions in suspending students for taking part in a lawful protest.

The anti-privatization protests at Sussex, and the manner in which the university's vice chancellor chose to respond to them, are symbolic of the way in which student political freedom is seen as beyond the pale in an increasingly marketized higher education sector. It is a form of behavior that is simply regarded as damaging to the reputation of the institution rather than being understood as students exercising a right to protest. The demonstrations were regarded as damaging to the reputation of the institution rather than being understood as students exercising a right to protest. It is significant that the anti-privatization protests at Sussex gathered support and public attention from a social media campaign. Students in higher education are encouraged to evaluate the quality of their teaching and other aspects of their 'learning experience' through completing course experience questionnaires and institution and sector-wide surveys, such as the UK National Student Survey for undergraduates. Yet, these questionnaire instruments impose strict confines within which students are allowed to evaluate. They are not the ones setting the agenda. Those who choose to go outside formal university quality assurance processes by venting their frustration or dissatisfaction online are regarded as dangerous mavericks.

Universities are keen to protect their institutional reputation and manipulate the outcomes of quality assurance to present their institution in the best light possible (Williams, 2010). They regard student criticism or actions outside of their own narrowly prescribed protocols as a threat to this institutional reputation. Institutions rely on the co-operation of the vast majority of students to maintain this image. From a pragmatic perspective, in a massified higher education system, it is not in the interests of students to take actions that might damage the reputation or image of their own institution (Rochford, 2014). Students who define their role as one of protest or resistance rather than compliance are seen as deviants for failing to see their role as one of self-commodification within the limits of how the corporate university defines and tolerates student representation and protest. The so-called 'student voice' is being domesticated by universities keen to protect the institution's image in a highly competitive higher education marketplace and by student organizations prepared to co-operate in neutering the role of student representation as a commodification of employability skills.

Conclusion

This chapter has highlighted the paradox that, while students now often enjoy high levels of personal freedom compared with erstwhile restrictions on their lifestyle and living arrangements, their political freedom is being redefined by institutions seeking to domesticate students within a marketized framework of student engagement. The constraints that affected the private lives of students like Ted Turner may have all but disappeared. Yet, the extent to which students exercise political freedom is being curtailed as a result of self-commodification and the marketization of corporate universities that jealously guard their image and reputation in highly competitive higher education systems. This is a significant paradox that points to where one of the real issues affecting student academic freedom lies. While student political freedom will not form the principal focus of this book, its rapid domestication is a cause of serious concern.

Much attention has tended to focus on issues of personal and political freedom for students. Far less consideration has been lavished on how student rights are affected by the organization of teaching, learning and the curriculum. These conditions represent the day-to-day reality of a student's university experience but seem to have been comparatively neglected in the debate about student academic freedom. The next chapter will explore the growing impact of a pervasive culture of performativity and how this societal trend has had an impact on student life. This has, I will argue, damaged the extent to which students genuinely enjoy a freedom to learn in the university.

Chapter 4

The performative turn

The paradigm of distrust

In the nineteenth century, the English social theorist and utilitarian philosopher Jeremy Bentham produced a futuristic design for an institutional building called a panopticon. Although applicable to other types of institution, such as hospitals, his basic idea was for a prison that would allow jailors to observe the inmates without their knowledge. Part of the idea of the panopticon was that it would be a more efficient means of managing a prison since it would require fewer staff to observe and control the prisoners. This was partly facilitated by the circular design of the building and by the mental uncertainty felt by the inmates who would never know when they were being observed.

In the twentieth century, the French philosopher and social theorist Michel Foucault used the panopticon as a metaphor for the way in which hierarchical organizations within society, such as the army or factories, use technology to observe and control human behavior (Foucault, 1977). The growing pervasiveness of technology means that panoptic structures have appeared almost invisibly in contemporary society but at an alarming speed affecting people's everyday lives. Photographic surveillance is commonplace. There are closed circuit television systems in city centers, workplaces that monitor emails sent by employees and identity cards that can recognize biometric data. Making private information public through social networking sites has become an everyday feature of modern life. What used to be thought of as private is rapidly being transformed into something that is shared in the public domain.

We live in a society where our movements, transactions and activities are increasingly observed and analyzed. Governments and commercial organizations are hungry for information about who we are, what we think and how we behave. This data collection process means that businesses are beginning to be able to predict what we are likely to next buy before we actually do so ourselves. You order a book online and then, a few weeks later, receive an email from the company suggesting that there are other products you might also want to purchase. Our habits, desires and weaknesses are analyzed as a means to try to maximize how much money we might spend on goods and services. We are being watched and our movements, physical and virtual, are being constantly tracked. Our digital footprint is a rich source of information for governmental and commercial organizations.

The growth of surveillance in society is cause for concern among some and a source of comfort for others. There are essentially two sides to the argument. One emphasizes the positive safety and security benefits of surveillance while the other focuses on fears about the loss of personal privacy and the potential for those with this information to abuse their power. Security cameras in city centers are often justified on the basis of protecting public safety by helping to identity and catch those committing crimes or behaving in an anti-social or suspicious manner. Those that support surveillance measures tend to argue that anything that increases the detection of crime is justified and that only those with 'something to hide' need to be concerned. Critics that oppose the growth of surveillance see this phenomenon as undermining the right to privacy. Campaigners for personal liberty argue that things such as security cameras or identity cards erode rights to privacy in a free society. A further argument is that surveillance measures are based on a negative view of human nature and are indicative of a growing culture or paradigm of distrust.

The paradigm of distrust can be widely observed across society today and is pervasive in the university too. The nature of this distrust extends well beyond the conventional security cameras and swipe cards familiar in most workplace and business settings. Part of the change may be attributable to the massification of higher education. Students are no longer a tiny elite invited into a cloistered residential facility and enjoying, in extending this metaphor, a leisurely stay at a small private home with free run of the facilities. Their experience is now more akin to that of a customer staying overnight at a budget hotel chain where access to facilities is tightly monitored through security devices and even the clothes hangers are theft-proof. There is, in short, little or no trust at all.

This paradigm of distrust manifests itself in a number of ways. First there is a growing emphasis on compulsory attendance at university classes. Students are increasingly required to sign in, or even swipe in, to lectures using electronic readers installed in classrooms. This has been a requirement since 2012 for students attending any formal class, lecture or seminar at the University of East Anglia in the UK (University of East Anglia, 2015), one of several institutions to introduce this form of technology in recent years. Universities have developed these tighter attendance requirements in response, in part, to the arguments of the student engagement movement (see later in this chapter) based on the rationale that students with better attendance records are more likely to do well in their studies and get a good graduate job. Much tighter rules have been put in place in respect to absences from class and the forms of evidence that are required by institutions to satisfy these requirements. Many universities even require students to produce a copy of a death certificate when absence is due to a family bereavement. Compulsory attendance at class is about what I call *bodily performativity* and will be explored in further detail, including the justifications for such rules, in Chapter 6.

There are numerous other measures demonstrating the way in which students are treated with distrust. Concerns about plagiarism are now central to assessment policies. While the word 'integrity' is used in these policies they are really focused on outlining the perils of acting without integrity, detailing how different forms of cheating behavior will be punished. Issued to students and explicitly discussed in induction programs for undergraduates, they are illustrative of the paradigm of distrust. The so-called Honor Codes or academic integrity promises that institutions ask students to sign up to are principally concerned with conveying a series of threatening stipulations about the perils of plagiarism. Most universities now use anti-plagiarism software as a means of supporting their so-called academic integrity policies. Students, from bachelors to doctoral degree level, are now commonly required to use this software prior to the submission of an assignment in order to check that their work is free from plagiarism. While the use of such software is often justified on developmental grounds by purportedly helping the student to understand more about good scholarly practice, reports generated by the software are now routinely demanded as evidence that the work being submitted does not fall foul of plagiarism rules. It has, in this way, become part of the surveillance culture at university and has even been extended by some institutions to proposals for doctoral study.

According to received wisdom, the internet has increased the prevalence of student cheating due to the ease with which published work can be subjected to 'cut and paste'. While an increase in cheating is often treated as a given, research has shown that such claims are exaggerated and that incidences of plagiarism have actually *fallen* among doctoral students since the beginning of the internet age in the early-to-mid 1990s (Ison, 2012). Plagiarism has existed since the dawn of time and is prevalent in the work of academic faculty as well as students. However, it is symptomatic of the way in which students are treated as inferior members – or, perhaps non-members – of the academic community that, while their written assignments are routinely scrutinized for signs of plagiarism via popular software packages, the papers that academics submit to journals and publishers are rarely subject to the same kind of rigorous tests. Another illustration of this double standard is that students are punished if they fail to list sources of evidence in their work and yet professors often adopt a much more lax attitude in presenting their own lecture materials.

There is a tendency for plagiarism to be treated as a catch-all for a wide range of incidences of poor scholarship spanning everything from stealing a piece of work in its entirety and claiming it as one's own to sham paraphrasing, the latter occurring where insufficient skill is applied in expressing the ideas of another using different words (Walker, 1998). Treating this wide gamut of behaviors as equally devious, as research studies and policy statements often do, fails to take account of the circumstances and relative level of experience of the student as a writer or understanding of the academic conventions of the discipline. A major study of plagiarism across 27 European countries concluded that, in the opinion of bachelor and master's level students, academic faculty, senior managers and administrators responsible for quality assurance policies 'the majority of student plagiarism is accidental' (Glendinning, 2014: 14). It is little wonder that heavy-handed plagiarism policies strike confusion and fear into a large number of students (Gullifer and Tyson, 2010) particularly those writing in their second or possibly third language who do not possess the expected level of understanding about the academic writing genre (Abasi and Graves, 2008).

Not content with the routine use of anti-plagiarism software and asking students to sign up to Honor Codes, universities often further require students to declare that each individual assignment they submit is free from any form of dishonesty. At one level, such a requirement might be justified on the grounds that only students with something to hide need to be concerned. Yet such a justification is much the same one as used to justify the use of hidden cameras in the high street or even in the workplace: that only the guilty have anything to fear. Requiring such declarations is designed to intimidate and spread fear and demonstrates a *prima facie* assumption of distrust. It is clearly overkill on the basis that students may have already signed the Honor Code or been issued with the plagiarism regulations of the university.

In the online learning environment the digital footprint of the student is now tracked via learning analytics. Here, data is gathered from course management and student information systems with the purported intent of improving student success. Computer-mediated communication is often used to encourage collaborative learning via discussion forums, although the number of postings to such forums is not necessarily an indicator of the building of a strong community, particularly where a large number of posts receive no reply (Dawson, 2006). The technology further means that students can be tracked every time they log in to a university system, including the number of times they interact via sending messages or comments in online courses. These interactions may be subject to interpretations with respect to the 'time and effort' that they have devoted to their studies. Online technology is further deployed to detect any 'inappropriate' (i.e. deviant) written contributions to discussion forums. This allows teaching faculty to approve or block such contributions before they are even posted which means that, unlike in the face-to-face classroom environment, student contributions can be censored before they are broadcast on the grounds of the use of 'inappropriate' language or the expression of views considered as prejudicial to a tolerant learning environment. The control and censorship of student contributions to online forums in this way is normally justified on the basis of preventing 'flaming' where exchanges can degenerate into a series of impolite or abusive comments. The fact that the design of such online systems allows the university, as a central authority, to watch students in this manner is clearly a further illustration of Foucault's panopticon at work (Slade and Prinsloo, 2013).

The audit of learning

There are other ways in which Foucault's panopticon has traction as a metaphor in university life. One of these relates to what is known as the audit culture. We live in a time when more people than ever before lay claim to a professional identity or status. It is no longer a nomenclature reserved solely for physicians and lawyers. There are engineers, accountants, teachers, nurses, bankers, librarians, dentists and even marketing professionals. It is ironic, though, that while the ranks of the professions may have swollen, their relative autonomy has correspondingly shrunk. Schoolteachers arguably enjoyed a higher degree of autonomy in relation to their practice before the professionalization of their occupation. This is because governments around the world have become more prescriptive about both what is learnt, through a national curriculum, and how it is taught, through increased scrutiny of teaching methods.

Professional self-regulation has given way to a new era of accountability. This means that professionals must provide evidence that they are performing well: keeping their knowledge up-to-date, caring for clients properly, using their power and status appropriately and, particularly for those in the public sector, demonstrating that they are providing value for money. Trust been displaced by what has been called an 'audit explosion' as the principles of financial auditing have been transferred to other professional contexts, such as higher education and medical services, and used to evaluate non-financial activities (Power, 1994; 1997). It is not an exaggeration to state that auditing, monitoring and evaluating have become terms as familiar to a higher education professor as to an accountant.

This trend can be understood positively as indicative of a society in which the average citizen is better educated and less deferential. Specialist information, once the sole preserve of professionals, is now more freely available via the internet. There is a plentiful supply of websites devoted to helping people avoid the need to consult a professional at all: diagnosing your own medical problems, drawing up a will, applying for a divorce and so on. People no longer have blind faith in professionals. A further argument is that governments must play an active role in ensuring that professionals, particularly those in receipt of public funding, are doing a good job. They need to do this in order to properly respond to the concerns of stakeholders, especially the taxpayer. Unless standards of performance are more closely monitored and scrutinized, how, it may be asked, can we expect to raise the quality of services? These arguments seem, in many ways, entirely reasonable.

The growth of the audit culture, and the reduction of professional autonomy that has gone along with it, may be viewed, less positively, as symbolic of a loss, or a crisis, of trust (O'Neil, 2002). Professionals can no longer be trusted to regulate themselves or be assumed to be acting in the interests of their clients or the wider public. Instead they need to be closely monitored to ensure that they offer value for money and conform to a series of performance-based targets.

In response to increased regulatory pressure, professional bodies have produced codes of conduct or statements of ethics, or considerably expanded earlier iterations. These codes have become ever more detailed, correspondingly diminishing the room for professional judgment. The loss of autonomy tends to erode a professional's sense of their own agency and, in turn, the extent to which they are likely to act in an ethically responsible manner (Solbrekke and Sugrue, 2011). Ironically, it worsens rather than improves their professional behavior. Rather than internalizing values as part of a sense of their identity, professionals now understand them as merely an externally audited element of their practice. Nowadays professionals must operate according to a series of regulations and protocols and meet standards against which their performance is evaluated. This, again, might seem perfectly reasonable but here there is a real risk that meeting the performance standards starts to become an end in itself rather than a definitional guideline. Rewards and punishments can be crudely linked to professional standards and begin to distort the activities and purposes of professional life. This is when 'performativity' takes hold.

In higher education, performativity is recognized for the way it increases the workload of academics in complying with audit and self-reporting procedures in respect to both teaching and research. In the UK, Australia, New Zealand, Hong Kong and other contexts internationally there has been increasing emphasis on the measurement of research quality, a process that began in the UK in the mid-1980s. The financial costs of these quality audit exercises alone are estimated to outstrip any benefits that might have been derived from them (Brown, 2013). Despite the evidence of the financial costs and the distorting effects on academic life caused by research audit exercises, there are now moves afoot to extend the use of metrics in relation to teaching too (DBIS, 2015). Performative teaching implies that it meets certain measurements that are endorsed by audit and quality control mechanisms (Skelton, 2005). At the institutional level, UK universities are expected to demonstrate that their teaching and student learning is at a high standard through metrics based on destination statistics about graduates, data about student retention and continuation, and the results of the National Student Survey, a university course experience questionnaire aimed at undergraduate students. In the future, pressure to demonstrate that institutions are offering good 'value for money' is likely to increase. A UK government Green paper published in 2015 (DBIS, 2015) includes a measurement of 'teaching intensity' suggested as a measure of the time students are studying plus the amount of time academics spend teaching. It may seek to measure 'work readiness' skills designed to make students more employable. Conforming to the demands of these current, and likely future, demands absorbs considerable attention and energy that arguably might be better spent focusing on actual professional practice in research or teaching.

Yet, the loss or lack of trust experienced by the professoriate in the way in which their teaching and research activities are now evaluated extends to the treatment of university students too. They are now as much the objects of performative expectations as their professors. This can be observed in a variety of ways: through the growth of attendance registers accompanied by more punitive university regulations, the grading of contributions in class, the use of methods of assessment designed to ensure student presence in class, the extensive use of anti-plagiarism software, and the organization of the teaching and learning environment to inculcate students with the skills and values that meet the demands of the audit culture. This might be described as the audit of learning. Many of these instances of student performativity will be picked up in more detail in the three chapters that follow this one.

Conventionally, a student's 'performance' at university is associated with formal, individual assessments leading to the award of a degree. Yet the trends identified so far in this chapter are part of a notable shift from the idea of learning as a private activity undertaken by a student reading for a degree, to one based on giving a public performance (Macfarlane, 2015a). The assessment of learning has become increasingly focused on a student's behavior rather than their cognition. In a performative environment knowledge is understood, not as the search for truth or individual meaning, but as an input and output measure (Lyotard, 1984). This means that, in common with their professors, students must focus on giving a 'good performance' that satisfies the measures used by the audit. In contemporary society this is how knowledge is legitimized. Being a student in higher education increasingly requires a 'performance mode' (Kettle, 2011: 4). Students must be prepared to enter into class discussions, take part in collaborative group work and make oral presentations. There is an increasingly censorious attitude toward learning in a private mode of individual reflection and contemplation and exercising choice about whether or not to speak. Staying silent is no longer an option. Students need to be *seen* to be learning. Performative expectations have profoundly changed what it means to be perceived as a successful higher education student. The way in which university students are evaluated now increasingly involves an assessment of their social and behavioral skills and attitudes rather than their intellectual understanding and achievements. It increasingly involves patterns of compliance that seek to assess academic non-achievements. This needs to be understood as part of the university's new 'hidden' curriculum (see Chapter 1).

A feature of performativity is that it highlights the importance of some aspects of academic work (e.g. research output) but renders other non-audited elements (e.g. personal tutoring or service activities) almost invisible (Murray, 2012). Service or academic citizenship components of the academic role are threatened by the way that performative measures are focused on publication targets, income generation and teaching evaluations via course experience questionnaires. It is only rational that academic faculty should put their energies into meeting these targets at the expense of activities that are not measured and, therefore, valued. In parallel, students are now expected to demonstrate more visibly that they are 'learning' rather than simply being offered the opportunity to attend lectures and seminars. The results of their intellectual endeavors undertaken in private need to be packaged in a manner that can be observed, through oral presentations, class contributions and reflective assignments. Those better able to comply with the demands of this behavioral audit will be the winners, while those without these skills are regarded in a negative light as passive learners and their grades may well suffer as a consequence.

It is important to understand how and why the audit culture has become part of the fabric of higher education systems. In *The Audit Society*, Michael Power (1997) identified two organizational responses to the auditing of their activities. The first, drawing on the work of Meyer and Rowan (1977), is called decoupling, whereby organizations seek to contain the effects of external audit by compartmentalization. They establish specialist units and appoint personnel with the objective of meeting the demands of the audit while, at the same time, trying to protect or buffer others within the wider organization from the effects of the audit. This is why universities have invested heavily in quality assurance units and appointed staff whose task it is to ensure that the institution is conforming to the audit demands of government funding agencies and professional bodies. Appearing at the other end of the continuum, colonization (Power, 1997) represents a wholly different response to audit. Here, the mentality of the audit culture penetrates the organization so deeply that its assumptions become embedded and widely accepted. University global rankings have moved into the mainstream of academic debate and are now widely accepted as legitimate measures of international prestige by most universities. The colonization of the audit culture is, in several respects, more notable in respect to student rather than teacher performativity. The latter is still widely characterized as an unwarranted assault on the professionalism and autonomy of academics. By contrast, the former is generally viewed positively as contributing to higher levels of so-called student engagement at university.

The student engagement movement

The growing emphasis on student performativity needs to be understood in the context of the rise of the student engagement movement. In the 1980s and 1990s universities developed internal student feedback systems in response to increasing demands for quality assurance data. The effects of the audit culture within universities progressed from responses based on de-coupling to that of colonization. Now quality was, to use the slogan, 'everyone's business', not just that of the quality assurance unit. While quality assurance systems were at first resisted, they have subsequently become institutionalized. Government and other national-level quality audit instruments started to emerge, increasingly linked to performance measures in relation to student retention and achievement. The National Survey of Student Engagement in the US was introduced in 2000 and versions of it have subsequently been adopted in most developed higher education systems, including Australia, Canada, South Korea, China, Japan, New Zealand, Mexico, Ireland, South Africa and the UK (Coates and

McCormick, 2014). One of the drivers for this is that mass higher education systems are associated with high levels of non-completion and student engagement initiatives have evolved, in part, to ostensibly improve student completion and success rates at university. Higher education institutions often have their own programs in place, such as The Student Success Program (SSP) at the Queensland University of Technology in Australia. This is designed to identify and support those students deemed to be 'at risk of disengaging from their learning and their institution' (Nelson *et al.*, 2012: 83).

The phrase student engagement is contentious and is used to mean a variety of things but is strongly associated with a learning environment where participants, drawn from diverse backgrounds, are actively engaged in a participatory culture and experience an adequately resourced and interactive approach to teaching (Newswander and Borrego, 2009). While establishing a commonly accepted definition of student engagement is challenging, internationally attempts have been made on the basis of substantial literature reviews. Trowler's (2010) review for the Higher Education Academy offers the following definition that recognizes both the participatory nature of student engagement and its intimate link with student learning gain and institutional efficiency:

> Student engagement is concerned with the interaction between the time, effort and other relevant resources invested by both students and their institutions intended to optimise the student experience and enhance the learning outcomes and development of students and the performance, and reputation of the institution.
>
> (Trowler, 2010: 3)

A systematic literature review of over 21,000 publications in a higher education context has similarities in placing a strong emphasis on this notion of a participatory learning environment:

> The concept of student engagement suggests positive involvement in programmes through active participation and interaction at a class level. Often underpinning this assertion is the assumption that any activities that get students more involved are a positive step towards improving the quality of student learning.
>
> (Evans *et al.*, 2016: 10)

The same study used a more focused sample of publications to identify the pedagogical approaches most closely associated with the promotion of student engagement. This revealed that 25 percent of articles made reference to active approaches to learning while a further 26 percent alluded to collaborative, co-operative or group-based activities. Hence, student engagement has a strong behavioral dimension that demands in-class participation. This is at the heart of student engagement at the classroom level. The emphasis on active learning is unsurprising given that the expression 'passivity is the enemy of [student] growth' has become practically a mantra of the student engagement movement for those that subscribe to its principles (Coates and McCormick, 2014: 1). Second, the theory of student engagement has an emotional element in the way that students are expected to relate to others and to their learning environment, and, third, a cognitive dimension representing how students should construct their own understanding and learn how to learn more effectively (Fredricks *et al.*, 2004).

In short, students must demonstrate that they are 'invested participants' (Conrad and Haworth, 1997: 553). This implies a commitment to performative values such as learning co-operatively with peers, sharing their ideas in public forums, being prepared to take part in community-based projects and demonstrating a commitment to the normative values of social justice. In a survey of literature on student engagement in higher education, Kahu (2013) offers an analysis similar to that provided by Fredricks and colleagues (2004) by identifying three main perspectives: behavioral, psychological and socio-cultural while adding a fourth one, labeled as holistic. Kahu's (2013) conceptual framework for understanding student engagement lists the kinds of dispositions and behaviors expected of students matched to different educational purposes (i.e. affect, cognition and behavior):

> Affect: interest, enthusiasm and belonging
> Cognition: deep learning, self-regulation
> Behavior: time and effort, interaction, participation
> (adapted from Kahu, 2013: 766)

The assumptions that inform student engagement are that anything that gets students more involved in participating at university is a good thing. It makes the process of learning more communal and, furthermore, is underpinned by the pragmatic arguments that, if students are engaged as learners, they are more likely to complete their studies, obtain better degree results and gain life skills suitable for the employment market (e.g. Allen, 1999; Astin, 1993; Kuh *et al.*, 2008). Hence, student engagement theory and university initiatives see performativity in a positive light as contributing to learning and improving completion rates. They are stubbornly blind to the anti-libertarian implications of performativity. A key assumption of advocates of student engagement is the idea that students should be rewarded on the basis of what they are *seen* to be doing rather than necessarily on what they are achieving intellectually. McCormick and Kinzie (2014: 14) offer the following definition of one of the central purposes of student engagement: 'The first is the amount of time and effort students put into their studies and other educationally purposeful activities.' This emphasis on 'time and effort' is reflected in the British government's proposal for a teaching excellence framework in its 2015 Green paper that defines student engagement in terms of 'student effort', 'learning gain' and the acquisition of 'work readiness' skills (DBIS, 2015: 32, 25, 11).

The rise of student performativity may, in part, be explained by the expansion of vocationally oriented subjects within the university curriculum placing more emphasis on the public testing of professional skills and the development of behavioral values associated with the workplace. This has increased the proportion of university professors teaching these subjects, often bringing with them a set of performative expectations from professional and workplace settings that are then transferred into the curriculum. The importance of students demonstrating competence in various aspects of vocational and professional practice has led to approaches to assessment that place more emphasis on demonstrating the acquisition of work-based skills and dispositions.

Student performativity has a number of interconnected elements – behavioral, emotional and cognitive (see Table 4.1). The rise of social constructivism has led to a tendency to valorize forms of learning that are active, social and interactive. Such forms of learning can be more easily observed and measured in attempts to build evidence for so-called student engagement. The word 'passive' has become almost a pejorative term negatively labeling forms of learning that are individual and introspective in nature, such as reading, listening or silent observation. This marks a further shift from understanding learning at university as taking place principally in a private space to something that is increasingly expected to occur in a public one.

Encouraging inauthenticity

The performative environment demands that students must play the role of the engaged and attentive learner. They must further conform to the demands of emotional performativity by entering into a 'confessional' style of learning through reflective exercises or demonstrating commitment to global social issues through service and experiential learning initiatives. Students are encouraged to capitalize on all aspects of their formal and informal learning in order to promote perceptions of their suitability for employment. Here, there is an emphasis on putting the emotions center stage by presenting the 'right' values and attitudes.

Table 4.1 A model of student performativity

Type	Signature pedagogies	Examples of assessment
Bodily performativity	Compulsory classes (e.g. lectures, seminars, etc.)	Attendance grading Attendance proxies (e.g. in-class tests)
Participative performativity	Whole class discussion Group and peer learning Debates Online discussion boards	Class participation grading Graded group assignments Oral presentations
Emotional performativity	Experiential learning Service learning	Self-reflection exercises (e.g. reflective journals or diaries; positionality statements, etc.)

This introduces a pressure to make disclosures about personal beliefs that some may experience as an invasion of their privacy. Such requirements further run the risk of encouraging inauthenticity as a means of coping with such demands. Academics and students need to do so in word as well as deed. It requires learning how to 'play the game' as individuals endeavor to conform to this agenda. Those who resist are subtly disadvantaged. Students who remain silent in seminars or do not participate sufficiently in online learning communities risk losing out when class participation grades are awarded. Those that fail to use the right lexicon, prefer to keep their emotions private or do not capitalize sufficiently on opportunities to wear their heart on their sleeve in describing their emotional reaction to new knowledge or an incident in professional practice may be similarly disadvantaged.

Hence, impression management is key to performativity. Here, student performativity needs to be understood by reference to existentialism and the dramaturgical metaphor. Goffman (1959) identified the role of performance in social interactions and how this invariably involves efforts to create the right impression. Performativity is often connected with playing gender roles but it applies to any social role including, by extension, being a student. This means, in effect, that students have to increasingly *perform* learning, something that Sartre recognized only too well: 'The attentive pupil who wishes to be attentive, his eyes riveted on the teacher, his ears open wide, so exhausts himself in playing the attentive role that he ends up no longer hearing anything' (Sartre, 1956: 60).

While Sartre argued that individuals are really free to act as they choose they often find themselves effectively imprisoned in roles. University students find themselves increasingly trapped by the demands of the student engagement movement. Students must play up to a series of behaviors that they are expected to act out – keen attentiveness, respect for authority, a love for the subject, an enthusiasm for learning, and what is judged to be the possession of a social conscience – the hidden curriculum of the age. Where individuals play up to behavioral expectations they are forced to restrain the expression of emotions and conceal actions that are inconsistent with the ideal performance (Goffman, 1959). This involves diverting a considerable amount of effort from actual learning into the performance of learning. Conventionally, in the context of student learning, performativity is associated with girls or young women hiding their intelligence and playing a more passive role in class in order to conform to a gender stereotype not to appear *too* intelligent in front of boys or young men. They seek to present an 'idealized' image of themselves from a conventional male perspective, one that is not too intellectually powerful. Yet, the implications of student performativity apply to all students at university.

The assessment of student learning is an area that has been perhaps most significantly affected by performative expectations. This has led to students being increasingly assessed on the basis of their academic 'non-achievements' (Sadler, 2010: 727). These are behavioral or transactional incentives (credits and penalties) and include grades for attendance at class. The time that a student spends in class is a non-achievement, not an academic one. Here there is a parallel with the time that a student has invested in seeking to complete an assessment task. Academics feel sympathetic and well disposed toward such students for doing their best. Yet, as Sadler comments (2010: 731), while their effort is commendable, this does not in itself constitute an academic achievement. The reverse of this situation is where a student produces a strong piece of work with an apparently low level of effort. The intuitive temptation of the professor might be to over-mark the poorly achieving hard workers and under-mark the lazy but more intellectually able. This is a timeless temptation. Yet, succumbing to it merely rewards academic non-achievement (Sadler, 2010).

The obligation to confess

We live in a 'confessing society' (Fejes and Dahlstedt, 2013), one in which Michel Foucault described Western man as a 'confessing animal' (Foucault, 1978: 59). As a consequence, becoming accustomed to writing in a 'confessional mode' and being prepared to self-disclose has become a narcissistic element of contemporary society (Lasch, 1979: 16). It can be found in the justice system, in medical practice, in family and personal health and counseling services, and daily in our newspapers and 'reality' shows on TV screens. Confession is closely related to therapy culture and a technology that is seen as central to fostering and maintaining good citizenship (Fejes and Dahlstedt, 2013). Emotional well-being has become a central concern of the therapy culture (Furedi, 2004). The mental health professions have expanded significantly and forms of therapeutic intervention, especially counseling, are now commonplace elements of human experience rather than something reserved for a small minority. Therapy has, in short, been normalized and schools and universities routinely employ student counselors as part of their support services for students. Words such as 'stress', 'trauma', and 'self-esteem' have become an established part of the cultural vernacular (Furedi, 2004).

Within education, especially higher education, reflective writing has become the instrument by which confession has been legitimized as a learning technology. It is intended to provide an authentic insight into the links between professional theory and practice; a window into the inner thought processes of students. Assessing reflective writing brings to the fore performative rituals of confession and compliance (Ross, 2011). Bleakley defines the reflective journal as a 'personal-confessional' based on a 'discourse of self-surveillance' (2000: 16). Students must display a range of emotional responses in their reflective writing: penitence for past mistakes or lifestyle choices and excitement and gratitude for the way an incident or experience has 'transformed' their lives. The idea is that confession can strengthen self-awareness.

Reflective writing practices have become an important element of student assessment, particularly in postgraduate professional and vocational courses influenced by the work of writers such as Schön, Dewey, Habermas and Kolb

(Ross, 2011). In a higher education context, the work of David Schön (1983) has been especially persuasive. Reflective diaries and portfolios are now an established part of nursing, teaching, architecture and even accountancy courses. As one of the key concepts of teacher training in higher education (Kandlbinder and Peseta, 2009), reflection is an important part of an attempt to 'change academics' approaches to teaching from being teacher-focused to being more student-focused' (Hanbury *et al.*, 2008: 480). Reflection on practice is an integral part of the Personal Development Planning (PDP) initiative affecting all UK higher education students, not just postgraduates. Hence, the influence of reflection is widespread. The spread of reflective writing practices means that the emotions, or at least attempts to simulate emotional responses that may or may not be authentic, are now a central part of what is assessed at university (see Chapter 7).

Students can be strategic in knowing what the teacher's preferences are and 'audience-aware' in the way in which they produce reflective writing for a number of different readers (Ross, 2014). This engenders inauthenticity in complying with its demands of reflective writing:

> What are they looking for? They're looking to show that you've developed and that you recognise that you've developed, so that you can say 'This is where I was and this is the way that I've gone or the paths that I've travelled and the hurdles I've jumped over, to get to where I am now'. (Eileen, undergraduate)
>
> (Ross, 2011: 224)

Students in higher education are always anxious about what their lecturers or professors want from them. Understandably, this is something that they are constantly seeking to clarify. Those who promote and defend self-reflection might criticize this student's comment as a cynical or 'strategic' approach to reflection, one based on a crafty and inauthentic engagement. Students in higher education, though, are more likely to be motivated by a desire to succeed and to please, and may lack self-confidence. Students are in an unequal power relationship with their teachers as assessors of their academic work. The emotional performativity required of students through self-reflection statements is about the enactment of the performing self and shares a remarkably similar set of expectations to those imposed on reality television contestants required to demonstrate their emotional 'journey' (Macfarlane and Gourlay, 2009). They represent the 'surveillance of students' emotional and developmental expression' (Ross, 2011: 113).

Students understand that teachers are looking for a transformative story of their personal development, or better still, transformation from one set of attitudes to another. The more dramatic or transformative the story the more it might give the appearance of an opening-up of the self. It represents an ontological approach 'in order to correct distorted thinking about self' (Rolfe and

Gardner, 2006: 600). Here it is important to emphasize that this 'obligation to confess' (Foucault, 1978: 60) is not just confined to students in a few subject areas such as teacher education. It is applicable in all contexts in which the reflection is deployed as an assessed component of the university curriculum and is firmly established in social work and nursing degrees too (Gilbert, 2001).

Making capital out of doing good

The performative turn in university education means that students are under pressure to capitalize on all aspects of their learning in instrumental or economic terms. The massification of higher education in developed country contexts means that simply obtaining a bachelor's degree is no longer enough to secure a graduate job. Students must differentiate themselves from the crowd in order to get a good graduate job. Moreover, they need to do this while simultaneously coping with a considerable academic workload, trying to keep personal debt in check, and handling the expectations of parents or employers acting as educational sponsors. In a UK context, 1 in 5 parents with children under 18 say that they will pay the entire cost of their child's university education, currently estimated at more than £50,000 (LV, 2012). Most will contribute a substantial amount and less than 10 percent intend to make no financial contribution whatsoever.

On average, UK students spend around 30 hours per week studying for their degree (HEPI, 2013). Other studies indicate that students are working over 40 hours a week including class contact time and independent study (Kember, 2004). These figures take account of both scheduled teaching and the time students spend on their own additional private study, although there is considerable variation depending on the nature of the subject taken and which institution is being attended. A study of UK students estimated that they spend, on average, between 13 and 16 hours in private study (Dean and Gibbs, 2015), although such estimates are likely to vary across international contexts and by discipline.

A student workload of 30 hours per week, taking the most conservative figure, may seem perfectly reasonable and not at all excessive. Most people would regard this as a reasonably light working week but this is just student study time. Such figures do not take account of the fact that students are frequently working to support their studies as well as undertaking volunteering and extra-curricular activities. UK universities normally recommend that students undertake no more than 15 hours of paid work per week. The reality, according to survey data from the National Union of Students, is quite close to this figure and indicates that, on average, students work 14 hours per week during term time although around a third work considerably more (NUS, 2008: 33). Adding paid employment during term time to scheduled teaching and private study increases the average student's working week to around 44 hours. While a student may be formally defined as 'full-time' the realities of increasing student debt and the necessity of paid employment to alleviate their financial circumstances means that this has become something of a misnomer (Curtis and Shani, 2002). Instead, it is common for UK students to study and to work, on at least a part-time basis, in order to support their studies and minimize debt levels. Trying to combine term-time work with academic study is a cause of student stress (Watts and Pickering, 2000) and student counseling services report increasing demands for their services (Hoefer, 2013).

While part-time work helps students to alleviate some of the costs of their higher education, the nature of this work, both paid and unpaid, is especially important in shaping their future opportunities and building evidence to differentiate themselves in a crowded jobs market. Such awareness starts early and school children now learn how to create 'identities of success' based on the 'crafting of triumphant selves' (Keddie, 2016: 10, 12). This pressure continues into their university life as students in a variety of ways. Becoming a student representative is increasingly defined as an opportunity to develop a set of work-related skills such as participating in meetings, teamworking and negotiation (see Chapter 3). Self-commodification, defined as 'the pressure to turn one-self into a valuable product for the knowledge-based economy', has become the overriding concern of students in the final year of undergraduate studies (Roderick, 2010: 41). As an element of a de-politicized definition of student engagement, being a student representative is regarded as one of a number of volunteering and extra-curricular activities (ECA) that have become a key mechanism by which students seek to differentiate themselves from their peers. Studies indicate that the majority of students are involved in ECA, although disparities exist based on self-perceptions as to what activities constitute such work. Substantially more male than female students (76 percent compared to 48 percent) declare themselves as engaged in ECA although, when prompted, the gap is considerably smaller (73 percent compared with 60 percent) (Stevenson and Clegg, 2011: 46). Regardless of whether volunteering is motivated by civic consciousness or a desire to enhance employment prospects through self-commodification, such activity sends out a positive signal to employers which makes students more employable (Katz and Rosenberg, 2005). Educational organizations encourage students to exploit their voluntary and ECA and savvy students now routinely integrate mention of such work into their CVs or résumés and use it to differentiate themselves from competitors (Roulin and Bangerter, 2013). Volunteering activities have been converted into a performative measure demonstrating that students are committed to a set of dispositions and values considered a marketable benefit. This is yet another example of turning what was once formerly regarded as essentially private or personal information into performative data for CV-building.

Patterns of social advantage and disadvantage among students are played out in the way that those from wealthier backgrounds, or attending well-heeled universities, are often in a privileged position to build their CVs on the basis of their voluntary work through a study abroad program or going on a 'gap year', taking time out from study either immediately before or after attending university. Ostensibly, volunteering opportunities are seen as making a positive contribution in increasing global understanding and making a difference to people living in poverty. At the individual level they can be transformative experiences too, but they can also be advantageous in more instrumental economic and career terms. The phrase 'gap year tourism' is now used in the literature to describe a period of time in which an individual chooses to defer education or employment in order to travel (Millington, 2005). Although the concept of a gap year has existed for a very long time it is only comparatively recently that this has become 'professionalized' (Simpson, 2005). Gap years are now a vital marketable commodity that enables students to enhance their cultural capital and improve their employment prospects as a result (Lyons *et al.*, 2012). This means that being seen as a 'global citizen' pays a dividend in a competitive jobs market.

Lauding the extrovert

Performativity involves making the private public. Part of this trend involves a broader tendency within society toward a more extrovert, participative culture in learning and entertainment. In the sporting arena, spectators have become an audience while players are now often referred to as entertainers. 'New laddism' is an element of the changing face of spectatorship in international cricket where, over the last 15 years, the so-called 'Barmy Army' of travelling England cricket supporters have challenged and altered the more reserved tradition of English cricket-watching (Parry and Malcolm, 2004). Fancy dress competitions among spectators at international cricket matches held in England are now common and encouraged by match sponsors. Extrovertism is legitimated and rewarded as the crowd becomes as much part of the entertainment as the game of cricket itself. So-called crowd-based performative interaction, such as the 'Mexican wave', may be found both at sporting events and at music festivals (Sheridan *et al.*, 2011). In culture and the arts participation is on the rise. Visitors to museums no longer simply gaze at the exhibits; they interact in the 'participatory museum' (Simon, 2010). This trend may be seen in alternative protest and art forms such as flash mobs that can constitute both a form of street entertainment and, potentially, a more radical form of 'performative resistance' in response to governmentality and the control of society (Walker, 2011: 3).

The counterpoint to the shift to a more extrovert society is that shyness is now regarded as tantamount to a deviant behavior (Scott, 2006). Those who decline the opportunity to join in with the Mexican wave are mocked as social misfits and 'spoilsports'. Those that complain about lewd or loud behavior at a cricket match are similarly mocked as 'party poopers', but being reserved or having a lack of social confidence has not always been seen as a social stigma. Particularly for women and young children it has conventionally represented behavior considered 'cute' or 'endearing' (Scott, 2006). For men, though, shyness was seen as more of a problem where it acted as a barrier to them forming intimate heterosexual relationships (McDaniel, 2001). In contemporary Western society, shyness is further seen as a problem for both men and women due to 'the increasing pressure to be ambitious, assertive and communicative' (Scott, 2006: 138). It is regarded as a social disadvantage for both sexes in achieving a healthy relationship and a successful career. In short, shyness is now defined as a form of social deviancy.

The flip side to the medicalization of shyness is the lauding of the extrovert or what Susan Cain refers to as the extrovert ideal (Cain, 2013). In the contemporary classroom, those that speak up, ask questions, enter into debate and lead oral presentations are praised as 'active' and get rewarded for their contributions in class. Those that participate in ways that are not obvious or visible, such as via eye contact, note taking or active listening, are called 'passive'. Negative labeling of more-introvert and less-vocal students means that those who remain silent are accused of 'social loafing' (Latane et al., 1979). They are criticized as failing to contribute to discussion. Similarly, those who log in as members of online learning communities and read postings but choose not to write their own responses are condemned as 'lurkers' (Nonnecke and Preece, 2000). This judgmental labeling applies to individuals who read and observe but do not make contributions to oral or written discussion. Loafers and lurkers are branded as not just selfish but as borderline sociopaths who take without giving to the learning community. Shy students are seen as a problem in class and, allied to this assumption, there is plenty of advice and suggestions available for helping them to become more self-confident and vocal. A number of American universities, such as Penn State, Arizona State and Wyoming, even run speaking and reticence courses for students who are shy (Aviv, 2007). The existence of such courses demonstrates that shyness is now seen as a social problem.

Performative expectations centered on vocal self-expression have become central to student learning, a development that is tantamount to a moral panic (Cohen, 1972) that labels quiet students (and those that do not attend classes often enough) as members of a deviant group. They are regarded as a 'problem', inducing negative perceptions from university teachers who often assume that silence in class indicates a lack of interest or of preparedness to participate on the part of students. There has been a flip-flopping of assumptions about teaching. Silence in class is no longer seen as evidence of a well-behaved and respectful group of students listening attentively to a good teacher. Instead, such behavior is regarded as indicative of deviancy on the part of the student. The teacher is seen as a failure too, as being unable to promote an environment of active learning among students. Hence, students who are reluctant to participate in this manner are labeled as 'difficult' while their teacher is considered a failure for being 'teacher-centered'. While participation may be expected, or even demanded, students can sometimes feel uncomfortable in offering a contribution or opinion. Research has shown that this applies in online learning environments too, not just traditional classrooms (Gulati, 2008). Student silence may be taken as a personal affront by a teacher keen to conform to the doctrine of active learning.

Such reactions assume incorrectly that talking is essential to learning. Here, there is a need to recognize that listening and reflective introspection are legitimate forms of class participation (Reda, 2010). Silence can be just as indicative of 'a process of active engagement with the ideas of others' as talking (Reda, 2009: 59). Academic faculty, though, do not generally regard silence in such a positive light. They regard oral presentations as representing the highest level of class participation with attendance at class at the bottom end of expectations (Fritschner, 2000). Silence is not counted since any learning that might be taking place cannot be observed.

The pressure to participate is based, to a large extent, on Anglo-Western assumptions about the dialogic nature of the social construction of knowledge. This privileges the values of autonomy, oracy and critique, where the student is expected to co-construct knowledge with the teacher (Kettle, 2011). These assumptions have been applied to students from Confucian-heritage and other East Asian cultures with little attention to prevailing social values in these contexts (Harumi, 2010). Co-construction of knowledge sometimes conveyed by the phrase 'student as co-producer' has become a fashionable idea in Western higher education yet the assumptions that underpin this approach to learning are rarely challenged. While there are clearly well-established cultural differences in the way that participation in learning is understood, it is important not to stereotype Western attitudes any more than those of non-Western students. Chinese students are often stereotyped as quiet or shy learners in class, something represented as problematic in developing active approaches to learning. Much of the literature about Chinese and other East and South East Asian learners tends to focus on ways in which to encourage greater participation but the personality, not just the cultural heritage, of the learner needs to be taken into account. This means that quiet or shy students may be found among Western students with a preference for individual self-study rather than class participation or group work just as much as among those studying in other parts of the world.

The deviant student

Student deviancy in mass higher education covers a wide variety of behaviors regarded as demonstrating a lack of 'engagement'. In a teaching and learning context, this includes failure to attend class, showing a lack of enthusiasm (or of being 'in love' with the subject), participating insufficiently through speaking in class and questioning academic judgments with respect to grading. In terms of political freedom, deviancy has become associated with participating in non-violent forms of protest rather than capitalizing on the opportunities afforded by a formal student representative role to enhance a personal profile suitable for the jobs market (see Chapter 2). Deviancy has even been associated with students lacking social capital in the method they approach critical thinking in a way which is 'too critical or too opinionated' (Danvers, 2015: 9).

In the teaching and learning environment, the negative labeling of the shy or introverted and the use of terms like 'lurker' is part of a wider vilification of students who do not comply with performative expectations. The word 'feral', from the Latin for wild, is used in conjunction with the word learner to refer to students who are not easily domesticated by the demands and restrictions of the formal curriculum (Hall, 2008). Such students are seen as deviants as they are either unable or unprepared to comply with the expectations of the teaching and learning regime. Feral learners include both the highly gifted and those who are deemed to be 'at risk'. This euphemistic expression refers to students who are regarded as in danger of dropping out or failing. In higher education, concerns about students who might be at risk of failing have been used to justify the imposition of compulsory attendance requirements at university (see Chapter 6). While the motivation for such policies is often couched in terms of concern for students, the real reason is more pragmatic. Increasingly, higher education institutions are evaluated – and funded – on the basis of the retention of students. Allowing students to drop out can result in financial penalties imposed on universities. Funding and student retention are now directly linked in several university systems, such as Australia's (Asmar *et al.*, 2015).

The performative culture has a wider tendency to blame the student for failing to comply with its various non-academic demands. This tendency is closely connected to the argument that students now act like 'customers' in an increasingly marketized higher education system, an analogy used by a large number of writers and researchers (e.g. Delucchi and Korgen, 2002). This analogy has become a received wisdom in discussions about the nature of higher education. It has entered the lexicon and has brought with it a growing tendency to vilify students for acting 'like customers'. Students who request that grading decisions are reviewed have been pejoratively labeled as 'grade grubbers' (Delucchi and Korgen, 2002), a phrase that is particularly well known in a US context. 'Grade begging' and 'grade lawyering' are other negatively judgmental terms applied synonymously. Students are blamed for acting like consumers or customers yet the way in which they are treated by universities has only encouraged some, although by no means all, to think of themselves this way.

Yet, there is very limited evidence to support the popular trope that students behave like a customer, and in a manner that is considered disrespectful and even defamatory by some academics, in criticizing the quality of their learning experience at university. Such behavior, it is contended, damages the reputation and may even lead to the dismissal of academic faculty (Jones *et al.*, 2012). Such claims appear to be exaggerated. In a large-scale study, 30,648 student comments extracted from more than 17,000 course evaluation questionnaires showed that just 0.04 percent of them were considered to be 'abusive' and 0.15 percent of them were labeled as 'unprofessional' (Tucker, 2014). These figures do not constitute substantial evidence that students are acting as immature or aggressive 'customers'. If anything it shows the reverse of this claim.

Conclusion

This chapter has sought to set out the ways in which the performative turn has taken place in wider society and how these conditions now affect the student experience at university. The overriding rationale of the student engagement movement is how its policies and recommended practices, such as attendance or participation rules, impact on the quantifiable 'betterment' of student learning. The concern is purely on whether students learn more, achieve more, or improve their job prospects. The problem with this instrumental way of thinking is that it ignores the critical importance of student rights and student academic freedom. Some of the arguments of the student engagement movement, such as the centrality of student participation, choose to ignore evidence from the research literature on student learning. Yet, it is important to get beyond arguments about what produces the most effective learning environment and raise a different flag, that of a student's freedom to learn.

The effects arising from student performativity need to be understood in the negative way in which this agenda impacts on the rights of students as autonomous adults who have entered a voluntary phase of education – to choose how to use their study time, to learn as individuals, to speak or to be reticent and to develop their own ideas and values. These core elements of what it means to be a student in higher education are threatened by the performative culture giving rise to a number of key questions:

- How do expectations concerning narrowly constructed definitions of 'participation' at university impact on student academic freedom? Do students have a right to reticence, or even silence?
- How do attendance requirements affect the development of a student's autonomy and the extent to which they can exercise free choice?
- To what extent are students allowed to develop their own social values and attitudes at university? How does explicit promotion of the virtue of normative values impact on student academic freedom?

The three chapters that follow will seek to address each of these questions in turn. In doing so they will draw on Skeggs' (2009) analysis of how reality television programs symbolize the display of self-performance in contemporary society. Skeggs' work identified how participants provide a participative, bodily and emotional performance. University students enact a participative performance through a willingness to take part in learning processes such as group work and class discussion; a bodily performance by attending class, or virtually via online forums; and an emotional performance in respect to social values and practices demanding compliance and confession, examples of which include global citizenship in the curriculum and reflection on practice. I will refer to these three elements as participative, bodily and emotional performativity in the chapters that follow.

Chapter 5

Participative performativity

The 'dreaded group project'

'When I got out of high school and enrolled at the University of Alberta, I was particularly excited for one thing: the end of the dreaded group project. In high school a number of different things led me to hate working with others. We would prepare arbitrary presentations and our peers wouldn't listen to them anyway. I thought that studying English and Comparative Literature in university would mean never having to collaborate for meaningless group assignments again. Boy was I wrong. In fact, I seem to be doing more group projects than essays lately. When I first saw all the group assignment descriptions on my syllabi at the beginning of the year, I decided to be as positive as possible. Perhaps the maturity level of my groups would be higher in university. Boy was I wrong again. Group work only seems to get worse in university, and I can safely say that the biggest source of my school stress has come from working with my peers.

But instead of letting it get me down any more, I'm going to relive the worst group project I have ever been a part of and hopefully my misfortune will at least brighten your day. The final group presentation I did this semester was in one of my English classes. It was pretty straightforward: form a group of four, read an article in advance, prepare a PowerPoint presentation and speak in front of the class. I tried contacting my group a month in advance so we could coordinate what slides we wanted to do and how we wanted to present. Only one person answered. The other two ended up emailing me with just a week to spare. When I figured out what everyone wanted to present on, I made the Google Doc, did my part and waited. When I checked our project the night before, I noticed only one other person had started on it. The other two, again, had nothing.

Anxious, and paranoid that half of the group forgot about our assignment, I checked again the morning of the presentation. One of the two slackers had completed their part; the other group member still had done nothing. That person didn't forget, but just decided to leave it until the literal last minute. About 20 minutes into our presentation, our perpetually late group mate showed up – the Google Doc 'last edited' time showed it was because that person was still working on the slides – read that part and LEFT right in the middle of the presentation! The professor took marks *off for it. The project was worth about 15 per cent of the course grade and we all got the same mark.*

If you're one of those people who slacks off during group presentations, please pay more attention to them. For one, they're worth marks that can bridge the gap between an abysmal final grade and the one you truly want. More importantly, just because you don't care about your grade, doesn't mean you should diminish the hard work of your peers!'

This reflection on the perils of group work comes courtesy of a blog written by Ravanne Lawday, an undergraduate student at the University of Alberta in Canada. Her frustrations about the 'dreaded group project' and the slackers who contribute very little to it but still get awarded the same grade as everyone else are all too familiar to anyone with experience of teaching and learning in higher education. The usual practice in higher education is for teachers to award all group members a 'group grade' (Ko, 2014: 302). This is because they tend to focus on the product of their joint endeavors, such as an oral presentation or a written assignment or report, rather the efforts of individuals within the process, something that is more difficult and therefore more time-consuming to assess. It follows that in group projects 'the link between individual inputs and the output is not so clear; a "free-rider" might receive a high grade despite having little input in an otherwise good group' (Ko, 2014: 302). The reverse of this situation, where a hard-working student receives a lower grade than their individual efforts merit simply because they are a member of a weaker group, also happens, of course. This is why Ravanne Lawday feels unfairly treated.

The assessment of group work has grown in response to expanding student numbers and, partly as a result, the internet is full of gripes from students about the unfairness of group grading. Blogs and other social media commentary found on the internet is where students talk candidly about their experiences at university rather than in officially sanctioned course-experience questionnaires. This is where issues that *really* matter to students are discussed rather than the pet topics and set questions of institutions mindful of their reputation. It is authentic feedback. The concerns here focus on the fairness of handing out individual grades for group work projects, one of the issues that really exercise university students.

It is easy to dismiss Ravanne Lawday's complaint about group work as a sign of immaturity. Professors like to tell students that working with others and learning to be part of a team is a valuable workplace skill. The advice is normally much the same: 'It's tough but that is real life and you had better get used to it'. More sympathetic professors will make suggestions to improve communication and negotiation strategies with other group members, but essentially they are sugaring the same bitter pill. The common explanation – that in the real world you have to work with others over whom you have little or no control – has a ring of truth about it, but only up to a point. Yes, group work is important in work contexts, and conflict and uneven contributions do occur, but in real world contexts it normally involves hierarchical structures that act as a check on the behavior of free-riders content to let others do the hard work. Even without a group hierarchy, if someone is a free-rider in a workplace team news about their indolence or failure to co-operate with others is likely to reach the attention of someone in authority fairly quickly. It may then adversely affect their appraisal, promotion and even retention prospects. This reality means that free-riding is a much more risky behavior in a workplace setting than as a member of a peer group at university.

Student concerns about the fairness of group work is the kind of issue that is well known across mass higher education (e.g. see Flint and Johnson, 2011). Yet, it is not understood as a serious enough matter. Instead, the problems that occur in group work assessment are considered very much secondary to the benefits of co-operative or collaborative learning. This is widely perceived as critical both to the development of appropriate skills for the workplace and as congruent in getting students to learn actively and socially to construct meaning and knowledge for themselves. A social constructivist philosophy interprets knowledge development as an individualized process in understanding the world. This means that personal experience is as important as expert knowledge which has led to a tendency to emphasize the importance of students constructing their own personal understandings in a public way through social interaction instead of engaging with and acquiring knowledge as a private activity. The learner has become 'a do-er of learning' (Holmes, 2004: 627). The role of the teacher is, therefore, to facilitate student development rather than teach, as knowledge is no longer accepted as an objective construct.

The primacy of active and collaborative approaches means that issues of fairness or justice in allocating group grades or the rights of students to choose how they might wish to learn are seen as secondary considerations, if considerations at all. The phrase 'student-centered' is often invoked in connection with active approaches to learning that are intended to represent the polar opposite of so-called 'passive' approaches. Here, it is often assumed that students are learning passively if the teacher is talking, rather than learning actively through collaborative work and discussion with peers.

Student-centered is a term that was always intended to include, rather than exclude, considerations of rights and justice. It is about what is fair as much as about what 'works' or is 'effective' in terms of student learning.

In this chapter I will explore how the term 'student-centered', as defined by the American psychotherapist Carl Rogers in the early 1950s, has become widely accepted as a guiding principle in learning and teaching in higher education and used to justify what I call *participative performativity*. While the intentions of Rogers and other learning theorists was to develop a more democratic and liberating form of education, I will argue that the meaning of student-centered has morphed into a largely authoritarian construct in an era of mass higher education.

Understanding student-centered

Few would argue that education should not be student-centered. It might seem perverse to suggest otherwise. Indeed, in relation to teaching practice student-centeredness has become *the* guiding principle of learning theory over the past 40 years. The psychotherapist Carl Rogers derived the term from his exploration of a client-centered approach to counseling, arguing that, if the aim of therapy is to help someone deal constructively with their own life situation, then surely such a similar approach might be usefully applied to education (Rogers, 1951). In explaining how his view of education built on the concept of client-centered therapy, Rogers stated his first, and perhaps most famous guiding principle: 'We cannot teach another person; we can only facilitate his learning' (Rogers, 1951: 389).

This principle states that teachers should start by considering the needs and interests of the individual learner rather than their own agenda. Rogers saw the aim of education as the 'facilitation of learning' (1969: 105) rather than teaching. His argument was that there ought to be a shift of focus from teaching to learning. This is normally expressed as being 'student-centered' rather than 'teacher-centered'. In explaining a teacher-centered approach, Rogers parodies an academic faculty group tussling with the design of a new curriculum and squabbling over how they will 'cover' the course curriculum, avoid overlaps and divide up the content between different years of study. This, for Rogers, exemplifies a teacher-centered approach, one more attuned to the concerns and interests of the instructors in imparting information and ensuring that students reproduce what they consider to be the most important ideas when assessed. In explaining the term 'student-centered' Rogers identified many of the principles with which educators are familiar today: creating a permissive and non-judgmental classroom climate, promoting individual and group discussion, recasting the teacher as a facilitator and encouraging students to self-evaluate (Rogers, 1951). He further stresses that a student learns best when the educational process enables them to construct meaning for themselves.

The language used at both a national and an institutional level now largely reflects Rogers' emphasis on student learning rather than teaching. This shift is notable in comparing the discourse of two significant national reports on UK higher education: the Robbins report published in 1963 and the Dearing report which appeared 34 years later in 1997. As Barnett (1999) has identified, the Robbins report is mainly focused on professors in their role as 'teachers' and how they can potentially improve their 'teaching', and includes a chapter devoted to discussing these issues. By contrast, none of the chapter titles in the Dearing report contains either of the words 'teacher' or 'teaching'. Instead, it concentrates heavily on the 'learner', the importance of 'lifelong learning' and allowing students to become 'active participants in the learning process' (quoted in Barnett, 1999: 299). This report reflects the shift to what has become mainstream, signaling a privileging of the centrality of learning over teaching. As part of trying to rebalance the goals of academics and their institutions, the report recommended the establishment of an Institute for Learning and Teaching in Higher Education (which later became the Higher Education Academy) designed to help raise the status of teaching and establish university teaching as a profession. The reversal of the conventional ordering of the terms 'teaching' and 'learning' in the title of the proposed Institute were intentionally symbolic, placing learning *before* teaching.

Changing the discourse from teaching to student learning fits well with Rogers' principles but he was concerned about more than mere semantics and wanted students to enjoy the freedom to learn in the way in which they preferred. This was at the core of Rogers' theory and conveyed by the title of one of his books, *Freedom to Learn* published in 1969. He believed that it should be up to the student to determine the pace at which they learn, the academic level or difficulty, and how far they felt motivated to go in making progress (Rogers, 1969: 17–18). Hence, student-centered learning, according to Rogers, is fundamentally about giving students autonomy and handing them the power to make decisions about their own learning. It is about who controls the content of the curriculum and the pace at which students make progress. In *Client-Centered Therapy* (1951), Rogers had emphasized the link between student-centered learning and democratic principles, counter-posing these with a prevailing educational culture which he characterized as much more authoritarian or teacher-centered. He stated that 'the goal of a democratic education is to assist students to become individuals' (Rogers, 1951: 387), conveying his belief that the locus of control should be shifted from teachers, and their institutions, to the student.

For Rogers, student freedom was about the development of their 'inner autonomy' (1969: 271). This involved students having the courage to be free by developing their own personal meaning. He defined learning, to draw on the title of one of his other books, as about becoming a person. Rogers' vision of student learning was diametrically opposed to a behaviorist stance. The idea that behavior and change can be observed in the environment was, during the 1950s, the dominant school of thought in psychology represented by the work of Skinner, Pavlov and others. Rogers' thinking and writing was going against the dominant paradigm of his discipline by opposing this school of thought. He understood that autonomy in learning in its truest sense implies the right to make one's own decisions as an adult. This means that even choices students might make which teachers or educators may disagree with need to be respected. This includes a student's right to learn in the way in which they prefer. Rogers stated that, even if students wished to learn passively rather than actively, then this is a choice they should be allowed to make: 'If students are free, they should be free to learn passively as well as to initiate their own learning' (1951: 134).

Rogers sought to illustrate student-centered approaches to teaching by drawing on examples of courses designed by other higher education teachers that he respected. One of the courses he selected as an exemplar of what he felt was good practice was designed by Volney Faw, a teacher from Lewis and Clark College in the US. Professor Faw's course had a number of distinctive features, including giving students the option to select either individual or group projects, and to decide for themselves whether or not they wished to attend classes. Rogers quotes approvingly from the following passage of Professor Faw's course handbook:

> No penalty will be attached to missing some or all of the classes. As a matter of fact, students are encouraged to miss a class when they feel that the activity in which they are engaged is of greater psychological significance than attending a class session.
>
> (Rogers, 1969: 37)

It is clear that Rogers saw being student-centered as about respecting the choices and decisions of the learner even in situations where a teacher or educator might wish the student to make a different choice, such as not to learn actively or complete an individual assignment rather than participating in a group project. This is about real choice rather than imposing one mode or style of learning on all students. As Rogers saw it, each student had the right to learn in the way in which they preferred and should not be cajoled, coerced or otherwise pressured into engaging in ways they disliked. He understood student-centered as about student rights, not just about learning being more 'effective'. This is a crucial argument and one that is at the heart of my argument in this book.

It is important not to forget that Rogers wrote from the perspective of a psychotherapist. He derived the idea of student-centered teaching from identifying the importance of being client-centered in one-to-one counseling relationships. He recommended the use of a circle, commonly known as a teaching circle, as a desirable way to create an appropriate classroom environment. The circle was important to Rogers in establishing a relaxed, equal and democratic basis of class participation and physically symbolized the new role of the teacher as a facilitator or leader of discussion rather than as an authoritarian figure, but it needs to be understood that he was writing at a time long before mass higher education, when relatively small group sizes were common. Higher education teachers working in mass higher education systems do not have the luxury of small group sizes and intimate teaching circles. This is one of the significant challenges they face and why, to some extent, the voluntary nature of Rogerian principles have tended to be sacrificed at the altar of efficiency and learning gain.

The new ideology of learning

The work of Rogers has been profoundly influential in providing a foundation for understanding how to teach in a different way. The principles he outlined in respect to focusing on the needs of the students rather than the desires of the teachers are now widely accepted. Worldwide, universities espouse a commitment to a student-centered approach to learning (Frambach *et al.*, 2013). It is now commonplace to find references to 'learning and teaching' rather than 'teaching and learning' in all manner of university strategy documents, in the titles of those who hold senior responsibility as heads of educational development or associate deans, as well as in the nomenclature of educational development departments and course curricula. 'Learning and teaching' is now the conventional nomenclature. In the UK, the Million+ group of modern, mainly teaching-led, universities has asserted that its member institutions are at the forefront of student-centered teaching and that this approach 'reflects the aspirations of universities to have a transformative impact upon students by providing a learning experience that is dynamic, interactive and inspirational' (Million+, 2012: 6). Student-centeredness is the core principle that lies at the heart of popular approaches to learning and teaching including problem-based and experiential learning. In practice, student-centeredness in its true sense is only partially embedded in learning and teaching strategies and 'engagement' policies. These emphasize the need for students to participate actively in class rather than being passive learners (e.g. Penn State University, 2013). They do not reflect Rogers' more nuanced and democratic position that the wishes of each individual learner should be respected.

The training that university academics now receive on how to teach is largely shaped by principles derived from writers and theorists with a background in psychology, rather than drawing on theories and ideas from subjects such as sociology, philosophy, history and politics that are important in understanding teaching, learning and assessment in a broader socio-political context. Teacher training courses for university academics are based on a 'psychologised curriculum' (Malcolm and Zukas, 2001). It is another explanation as to why student rights, as opposed to 'effective' learning, are so low down on the agenda. The training of academics to teach at university is dominated by a small number of concepts drawn from the psychology of learning, notably student-centeredness and the importance of encouraging deep (as opposed to surface) learning (Kandlbinder and Peseta, 2009). This latter distinction is derived from the work of Marton and Säljö (1976) and is one of the five most influential concepts informing these courses (Kandlbinder and Peseta, 2009). The phrase 'deep learning' characterizes an approach to knowledge based on a desire to analyze, make links between concepts, and seek to explain and make personal sense of claims to knowledge. A 'surface' approach, by contrast, is associated with the opposite: acquiring a superficial understanding of knowledge, without a commitment to explore concepts in depth and doing just enough to pass examinations or other assessments. It is now practically an article of faith of such training programs that the teacher's energies should be directed at encouraging their students toward deep learning.

The adoption of a student-centered philosophy in the training of university professors might appear to bode well for the future of higher education. Programs unashamedly aim to 'change academics' approaches to teaching from being teacher-focused to being more student-focused' (Hanbury *et al.*, 2008: 480).

For the enthusiasts, student-centered learning is little short of a personal mission to change university teaching for the better, but these are often the same people who undertake research into student learning. This is reflected by the scholarship about teaching in higher education that is narrowly focused on identifying approaches to learning, measuring their effectiveness and applying them in practice (Howie and Bagnall, 2013). It reifies certain concepts and relies strongly on quantitative methods to seek to prove relationships between variables (Malcolm and Zukas, 2001). Learning is regarded as an inherently enjoyable and rewarding activity for students who are expected to be devoted to their studies, develop the ability to self-evaluate (Nicol, 2010) and be keen to understand its underlying concepts in order to adopt a deep rather than surface approach to learning.

Unfortunately, deep and surface learning has become an over-simplified moral dualism in much the same way as student- and teacher-centered (Macfarlane, 2015b). Being teacher-centered implies a selfish disregard on the part of professors for the needs and interests of students, while students who adopt a surface learning approach are similarly viewed as morally deficient in refusing to delve into their studies with sufficient interest, depth or academic commitment. They are unhelpful dichotomies in the sense that they imply that there is a right and a wrong way to teach and a right and a wrong way for the student to learn. The power of the deep/surface dichotomy has led to the negative labeling and blaming of students for using the 'wrong' approach when they prefer to surface learn (Case and Gunstone, 2003). For Rogers, surface learning would simply be regarded as a choice that a student has a right to make even if the teacher might prefer them to understand underlying principles and concepts in greater depth. It should not be a cause for some kind of moral censure.

There is a great deal of rhetoric about the importance of student-centered learning at university. Yet, Rogers' vision of what it means for a student to be free to learn has little to do with how students are treated in mass higher education systems. This is partly because the principles of student-centered teaching have not been genuinely realized and because institutions have created a learning environment which is increasingly dependent on surveillance and coercion. This authoritarianism is alien to the liberating ideal associated with being genuinely student-centered.

The inconvenient truth

The truth is that what Rogers meant by student-centered is now widely (mis) understood and incorrectly interpreted. It does not prescribe a one-size-fits-all approach to learning based on an active and participative classroom. The following are some inconvenient truths about student learning that are rarely taken seriously enough by educators committed to active learning approaches:

- Students prefer lectures with some limited interaction (such as question and answers) to more student-centered methods (Fusaro and Couture, 2012).
- Students' perceptions of teaching quality has an effect on whether they attend class (Kelly, 2012; Dolinicar, 2005; Dolnicar et al., 2009; Friedman et al., 2001).
- 'Surface' learning is essential to efficient time management and being in control of time (Case and Gunstone, 2003).
- Students often find working with peers a poor use of time and resent listening to dominating classmates (Hancock, 2004).
- Grading of group work is often seen as unfair by students (Volet and Ang, 1998; King and Behnke, 2005).
- Students often feel uncomfortable about sharing their opinions in class (Graham et al., 2007).
- Assessment criteria tends to mask 'hidden criteria' in the way that student work is graded on the basis of the amount of perceived effort (Sadler, 2010) or a student's likeability (Carless, 2015).
- Students feel anxious about the loss of anonymity in a large class when a 'student-centered' approach is used (Machemer and Crawford, 2007).
- Student-centered learning is based largely on Western values and assumptions (Asmar et al., 2015; Frambach et al., 2013)

The issues raised in this list are significant and generally well known, at least by researchers on learning and teaching in higher education. Yet, there is a collective reluctance to treat them as serious matters adversely affecting students and their freedom to learn at university. The difficulties connected with approaches to learning that demand all students to participate in active and collaborative classroom environments tend to be seen as little more than a minor inconvenience rather than having a significant negative impact on a student's freedom to learn. They are regarded as technical problems or side issues related to teaching and assessment techniques rather than as fundamental or significant challenges. This has brought about what Lesley Gourlay has termed the 'tyranny of participation' at university (Gourlay, 2015). A range of strategies are suggested for making group grading practices fairer, such as focusing assessment more on processes rather than the product. Much further discussion centers on whether to give students the choice in selecting group members. Yet, the principle of choice as to *how* to learn, argued for by Rogers, is rarely if ever invoked in these discussions. Discussion, instead, focuses on how to make a compulsory process slightly less unfair. The logic of the student engagement movement is that the effectiveness of learning, judged in terms of learning 'gain' and the relevance of group work in purportedly enhancing employability skills, is the primary consideration.

There are two reasons for the neglect of fairness. First, interpretations of social constructivism in higher education teaching mean that social interaction in learning is seen as sacrosanct. Social constructivism privileges the claims of personal experience over the knowledge of others with expertise. This rejection of objectivism means that student freedom is principally defined as stemming from allowing them the opportunity to construct their own understanding incorporating and legitimizing their personal experiences. Applied to all subjects across higher education this interpretation of teaching informed by the principles of social constructivism has the effect of undermining the role of the teacher or professor as someone who holds expert knowledge. Yet, even if the intentions are liberating, approaching teaching in this manner is not liberating for students if they are denied real choice as to how to learn. Individual students with preferences to learn in ways that do not fit the dogma of social constructivism are labeled as feral or in some way lacking in the right attitude to construct meaning in conversation or through interaction with others. The second reason for the neglect of fairness is that the student engagement movement is gripped by seeking to measure the effectiveness and efficiency of student learning rather than matters related to student justice. This belief, often expressed by those that write about learning theory, is that a teaching technique or tip will help to overcome any problem (or injustice) related to the assessment or pedagogic process. This is why concerns related to free-riders in group work assessment are not treated as fundamental problems affecting personal freedom and student rights but as technical glitches that can be addressed by monitoring group processes (Brown, 1994).

Narrow interpretations of social constructivism do not only dictate that students learn through interaction. These redefine the role of the teacher and, in the process, the importance of students constructing understanding of knowledge *for themselves*. Unfortunately, this is often confused with students entering into this process *by themselves* (Mascolo 2009: 7). Students should be afforded the support of the teacher and the intellectual space to come to their own conclusions about knowledge claims. Being student-centered should not be used as an excuse to send students away to learn by themselves without adequate guidance or support. Glibly telling students to 'take responsibility for your own learning' has become a familiar catchphrase and is sometimes used to justify a failure to offer sufficient learning support or scaffolding. Students are only too painfully aware of this problem in the way in which student-centered learning is applied in practice. Their main worry is that they will be told to 'just go away and find out without sufficient guidance, or before we have the necessary skills under our belt' (a student quoted in Lea *et al.*, 2003). Instead, as this student understands, they need a structure or scaffold by which they can learn independently, both with and without the teacher.

Being teacher-centered means the teacher has authority as the expert to communicate a specialist body of knowledge to students in a style in which he or she sees fit. This normally implies use of the lecture method in which the predominant role of the student is to listen while the teacher talks (Mascolo, 2009). The role of the teacher should be to encourage students to become deep learners rather than surface learners. Indeed, the censorious nature of phrases such as 'teacher-centered' and 'surface learning', implying, in effect, 'bad' teaching or learning, means that it is unfashionable to question the assumptions of social constructivism or the performative demands on students that follow. Curiously, while the phrase student-centered implies a self-conscious focus on the needs of students, the negative effects of participative techniques have tended to be overridden by arguments focused on the benefits students derive from achieving certain learning outcomes.

There is a wealth of evidence that students prefer to learn in ways that are often labeled negatively as traditional or passive, notably via the lecture method. In a study of 15,000 undergraduate students across several Canadian universities, Fusaro and Couture (2012) found that students prefer lectures, if they are engaging and relevant, to discussion-based activities. The research shows that instructors overestimate the extent to which students prefer this latter approach. This means that, while the literature emphasizes the superiority of active learning, students still rate lectures very highly and find elements of active learning, such as the time-consuming nature of these activities and the fear that they will not be able to cover the course material, disconcerting. Students like lectures to be interactive and engaging but defined in a relatively limited sense as those where the teacher makes a set presentation, students listen and take, or are given, notes and then have the opportunity to ask questions and perhaps undertake exercises to check progress (Sander *et al.*, 2010). They hope for, or prefer, an interactive lecture to other approaches such as student-centered teaching and group work.

Value for time

Ironically, the skills required to succeed at university, and beyond, can run counter to assumptions that deep, conceptual approaches to learning are superior to surface or strategic approaches. Time management is a critical skill in the information age. 'Fast' time is driving out 'slow' time (Eriksen, 2001). 'Fast time' refers to the displacement of time as a linear concept with 'stacking', involving simultaneous actions and processes. 'Slow time', representing uninterrupted periods where people can think and reflect, is especially important in academic life where learners must seek to understand and come with new ideas and experiences. The ability of individuals to manage this 'time tyranny', as Eriksen labels it, has become critical in a society which values efficiency above all else. Students (and academics) must cope with the demands of fast time and information overload in the same way as anyone else in contemporary society prioritizes tasks on the basis of their value for time.

As a result, rather than adopting a conceptual approach to learning, students more readily identify one based on their management of time. This can be represented as either 'being in control' or 'being out of control' of time (Case and Gunstone, 2003: 55). Students regard efficient time management as the most critical factor in determining their success. Undertaking activities involving deep understanding are often perceived to take up too much time and decision-making depends 'first and foremost on whether the task counted for marks and how much' (Case and Gunstone, 2003: 62). This strongly suggests that students approach learning in what is termed a 'strategic' way designed to maximize personal achievement (Kneale, 1997; Entwistle and Ramsden, 1983). A strategic approach to learning is really a variation on a surface approach since it is not principally focused on a deep conceptual engagement. While this is associated with students failing to engage adequately in understanding the underlying concepts of their subject, the ability to make discriminatory choices in how much effort to expend in the face of time pressure is a vital skill in the information age. University students are making a voluntary choice in deciding to use their time to study for a degree. They could use their time in other ways: for leisure pursuits, for spending time with their friends and families or for moneymaking activities, including full-time employment. Here, it is important to understand and respect the choices that students make in the way in which they choose to learn and their motivations for study.

A lack of value for time is one of the other reasons why students can resent group work. Such processes are lauded by those who argue that institutions should 'focus their efforts primarily on developing in students the ability to critically evaluate the quality and impact of their own work' (Nicol, 2010: 7). Yet there is evidence that students with predispositions to work alone can perceive time spent in discussion with peers as a poor return for time and resent listening to ill-informed and dominating classmates (Hancock, 2004).

There is more than a whiff of elitism about the insistence on deep learning. Demands that students should learn deeply and demonstrate enthusiasm for their studies are based on the assumption that there is something wrong with students who do not wish to explore the conceptual basis of a subject in depth. It is 'good for them' or self-evident. Yet, this is essentially an elite view of the purpose of higher education expressed largely by academics that write about and argue for deep approaches and find it difficult to understand why others may not share their level of passion for and commitment to their chosen discipline. They expect students to desire to learn deeply about their chosen subject as if they themselves wished to become academics. Perceptions about a lack of commitment to deep learning are often attributed to the effects of marketization on students but there is more than a hint of Golden Ageism in the idea that contemporary students are not as intrinsically motivated by their studies. This normally assumes that students used to be more self-motivated and less instrumental than previous generations. There is little evidence, though, to support this urban myth. Research published in the early 1970s, during a period of elite rather than mass higher education, asserts that students are not principally motivated by the desire for subject knowledge (Little, 1970; Startup, 1972; Wankowski, 1973). The reality of mass participation higher education systems in developed nations is that going to university has become a rite of passage for almost all reasonably well-educated young people wishing to enjoy a career in practically any white-collar occupation. It is no longer an option to apply without a university degree for most jobs with long-term career prospects. Employers treat a degree as a benchmark and will often not otherwise consider an applicant without one. Nearly all professional and para-professional occupations demand a degree qualification. Thinking that students are not as intrinsically motivated as previous generations is an illustration of the way an elite instinct still prevails in a mass system of higher education, as originally observed by Scott (1995).

The tyranny of participation

Participation is a central tenet of the new ideology of learning at university. Students must be 'active' and take part in collaborative and co-operative activities. Here it is widely argued that being an active participant will improve students' work-related skills along with their independence, self-motivation and critical thinking. There is a need, though, to look beyond the possible quantifiable learning benefits. Participation in active learning demands a *performance* on the part of students – to raise their hands, ask questions, engage in discussions and speak with their peers and teachers in whole class settings. The potential level of discomfort such demands make on students is something that is rarely taken seriously. Moreover, there is a tendency to falsely assume that it is only Chinese or other South Asian students that find the demands of participation difficult. Studies have shown that there are important differences in understanding the cross-cultural applicability of student-centered learning (Asmar, 2005; Asmar *et al.*, 2005; Frambach *et al.*, 2013).

The use of audience response systems has become commonplace in higher education classrooms. In a study of their use, getting on for a half of students (47 percent) were reluctant to share their own opinions publicly in class (Graham *et al.*, 2007: 245). The use of such systems is indicative of the emphasis now placed on eliciting responses from students, something that Carl Rogers opposed (see Chapter 8). Students are forced to risk embarrassment at getting an answer wrong or giving an opinion that they might rather keep to themselves. Even where responses are anonymized, peers will sometimes be aware of how other classmates have responded, particularly when allied with group processes. While teachers often assert that they make an effort to emphasize that student opinions are welcome and will not be judged as to whether they are 'right' or 'wrong' (e.g. Ni Raghallaigh and Cunniffe, 2013), this is essentially a teacher-centric perspective on creating a 'safe' learning environment. It does nothing to remove students' fears that they may be embarrassed in front of or subject to criticism from peers. One of the other consequences of asking students in a large class to learn collaboratively is that it forces them to lose their anonymity (Machemer and Crawford, 2007: 24). While confidentiality and anonymity are considered paramount in thinking about research ethics, such considerations are almost never extended to students learning in the classroom despite the obvious power imbalance. These are all reasons why students report feelings of anxiety and insecurity when teaching is organized in an avowedly student-centered way (Lea *et al.*, 2003) where 'student-centered' means using active learning for all, as opposed to respecting the individual preferences of learners. Expectations connected with individual participation and grading of such contributions ignores a student's 'right to reticence' (Chanock, 2010) and the role of silence in learning among students (Jin, 2012).

Group work has grown significantly in higher education in response to mass student numbers along with several other forms of continuous assessment (Richardson, 2014). As Ravanne Lawday's blog at the beginning of this chapter illustrates, students often view working and learning with others on group tasks in a less than positive light (e.g. Pfaff and Huddlestone, 2003; Ni Raghallaigh and Cunniffe, 2013). There are a number of issues that raise questions about both the effectiveness and the fairness of group work when such activities are assessed (Volet and Ang, 1998). Whether groups free form or are molded by the intervention of the teacher is one consideration. For instance, there is a noted tendency for home and international student clusters to segregate where groups free form without direction from the teacher (Wang, 2012). This can result in built-in inequalities in terms of the balance of expertise within groups.

Higher education has rapidly expanded internationally but often without a corresponding increase in public funding, leading to less well-resourced and larger class sizes, defined as anything between 40 to 80 students depending, perhaps to some extent, on the nature of the subject (Dixon, 1986; Buchanan and Rogers, 1990). This has increased the pressure on teaching and assessment. It is commonplace to acclaim group processes because they are said to represent how people work together in the 'real' world. They are considered as self-evidently justified on this basis. Yet, as pointed out earlier in this chapter, this is a misleading analogy as it fails to acknowledge that hierarchical relations play a critical role in the workplace and exact control over group members, aiding motivation for all individuals to contribute to tasks. This makes it much more difficult for a team member to freeload in the workplace. By contrast, on a university campus, all members of a group or team are peers without a hierarchical structure or reward and punishment mechanisms available to a group leader. This makes freeloading much more likely, especially if teachers fail to identify individual contributions to group tasks or allow groups to free form (Pfaff and Huddlestone, 2003). While strategies exist to make group work assessment fairer, it needs to be recognized that the popularity of this approach among most rank and file professors rests strongly on the perception that it will reduce their workload rather than improve student learning (Livingstone and Lynch, 2000).

A lack of transparency

When it comes to considering rights in the context of teaching and the curriculum, these are invariably interpreted in a one-dimensional fashion. In effect, pedagogic rights are seen as something that teachers possess rather than students, in much the same way as academic freedom more generally. The use (and abuse) of assessment criteria serves as a good illustration of the way in which the rights of students only appear to be served. Universities and quality assurance agencies claim that the adoption of assessment criteria in higher education proves that students are treated fairly. It makes the assessment process 'transparent' and 'student-centered'. Yet, the use of assessment criteria is far from a panacea. The complexity of language used to convey standards and difficulties in interpretation has long been recognized as a problem (Sadler, 1987; O'Donovan *et el.*, 2004). Research has shown that a student's 'likeability', rather than their actual academic levels of achievement, plays an important role in practice. Students can be downgraded by teachers who dislike them and correspondingly upgraded by teachers that consider them 'attractive' (Carless 2015: 166). Another element of what Carless labels 'hidden criteria' (2015: 166) concerns the variable interpretation of assessment criteria.

Perversely, writers and researchers on assessment often see this variation, which might otherwise be known as inconsistency, in a positive light as an assertion of a teacher's right to discretion and as about exercising 'freedom to interpret criteria according to their own values and emphases' (Carless, 2015: 166). The phrase 'academic judgment' is sometimes invoked but, in practice, this really indicates an assertion of academic power to make decisions without fully revealing the basis on which they were reached. In many respects assessment criteria provide academics with a convenient shield to protect themselves from any claims of unfairness; a series of bullet points, to hide behind. Ultimately, the self-justificatory nature of the way in which assessment criteria may be interpreted lies in the hands of academics.

It is not at all surprising that the UK National Student Survey for undergraduate students, first instituted in 2005, has consistently shown that students are less satisfied with respect to the fairness of grading and the information and guidance they receive about assessment than in comparison with other aspects of their educational experience at university. Improving the quality of feedback is seen as the main issue to be tackled by universities and assessment specialists. This has meant that, while a great deal of attention has focused on developing more detailed guidance and feedback designed to improve student understanding of academic requirements, far less thought has gone into analyzing why students think assessment grading might be unfair. This is largely because such complaints are simply treated as a barometer of student 'consumerism', not a legitimate concern.

Conclusion

Students do not always wish to learn through active and collaborative approaches and can be adversely affected by issues connected with their use. There is evidence that these problems exist, with reference made in this chapter to a series of 'inconvenient truths'. These issues though are viewed as unwanted or negative results when research into student learning is carried out rather than findings that positively support active learning initiatives. Here the possibility of reporting bias cannot be easily dismissed as researchers in learning and teaching are often strongly committed to an ideology supportive of active learning based on social constructivism. The scholarship of teaching and learning 'movement' encourages teacher self-reporting of practice-based research, normally within a framework of active and collaborative approaches within the curriculum. Other researchers occupy organizational positions both as academics and as developers with responsibilities for promoting the university's student engagement agenda. In all academic fields, research that casts doubt on received wisdom or argues against the dominant paradigm faces stiff opposition and this is no different in learning and teaching research.

While much of the rhetoric about being student-centered is now mainstream, the way in which students are treated in the university is not consistent with the principles outlined by Carl Rogers. Some of these principles, moreover, have been bent, or abandoned, to suit the needs of a mass system of higher education. A coercive version of student-centered has emerged heavily influenced by strategic and instrumental concerns connected with efficient use of teacher time and student completion rates. This has little to do with being student-centered as envisaged by Rogers and is more to do with measures designed to increase the efficiency of higher education institutions. This has had a series of adverse effects on students' freedom to learn through the way it demands participative performativity on the basis of observable forms of active learning and social interaction through group work.

Some of the problems with student-centered teaching are ones that Rogers himself identified, including the presence of students with a more instrumental attitude to learning and frustration about the value of group discussion. Open discussion was central to Rogers' vision of student learning and freedom but this vision was not based on the coercive use of class contribution grading or compulsory group work. Rogers characterizes a teacher-centered approach as one in which the operational assumption is conveyed by the phrase, 'you can't trust the student' and contrasts this with a student-centered attitude based on the opposite supposition – 'you can trust the student' (Rogers, 1951: 427). Sadly, higher education institutions demonstrate that they do not trust their own students. One of the most notable ways in which they demonstrate this absence of trust is through compulsory attendance requirements, a discussion about which will form the focus of the next chapter.

Chapter 6

Bodily performativity

'Go away, you're late'

In 2010 a student arrived an hour late for a brand management class taught by Professor Scott Galloway of New York University's Stern School of Business. The student was immediately told to leave by Professor Galloway whose 'policy' is to bar any student turning up more than 15 minutes late for class. The anonymous student later sent an email to the professor seeking to explain that on the evening in question they had attended lectures for three new courses in an attempt to decide which one to pursue. The one on brand management, taught by Professor Galloway, happened to be the third one they attended that evening and this is why they were an hour late. As the student had not been to one of Professor Galloway's classes before they were unaware of his policy on lateness. In response, Professor Galloway took the student to task for a lack of manners and respect telling the student to 'get your s*** together'. Keeping the name of the student in question anonymous, the professor then forwarded his email reply, via his teaching assistant, to the rest of the class.

Later the professor's email went viral on the internet. Reaction was largely favorable to Professor Galloway and his put-down even became a tongue-in-cheek motivational student motto printed on a T-shirt. Business Insider *magazine pronounced that the professor had given the student 'some valuable life advice' (Simoes, 2013). A number of commentators argued that the student had no right to be 'shopping around' to find the course that they liked best and that this behavior represented a consumerist mentality. Those who posted comments to social media sites criticizing the professor for his high-handedness were in the minority. Critics of his behavior mainly invoked the argument that students are now tuition-fee-paying customers and that the professor is offering a service.*

Stephen Fry's Cambridge

The English actor, director and comedian, Stephen Fry, went to Cambridge University to read English in 1978. In an autobiographical account of his early life, The Fry Chronicles *(2010), he describes his time as a Cambridge undergraduate. Fry's university experience was an elite one. He attended an all-male college at one of the world's most prestigious ancient institutions recruiting largely from privileged private schools. He was one of an intake of only five or six reading for a degree in English at his college, was taught in small seminar groups and, like undergraduates at Oxford and Cambridge universities to this day, enjoyed teaching terms lasting just eight weeks. This privileged position extended to students enjoying a 'healthy bank balance' (p. 72), at least at the beginning of the academic year. Being at university was as much about enjoying a social life as an academic one with Fry describing a social whirl of sherry parties, dining clubs, student societies and May Balls. His attitude to study was intensely intellectual but avowedly independent. He regarded lectures somewhat dismissively, as a largely redundant element of the curriculum and chose to attend very few of them:*

> *I only went to three lectures in my entire three years. I can only remember two, but I am sure I went to another . . . Lectures broke into one's day and were clearly a terrible waste of time, necessary no doubt if you were reading law or medicine or some other vocational subject, but in the case of English, the natural thing to do was talk a lot, listen to music, drink coffee and wine, read books, and go to plays.*
>
> *(Fry, 2010: 89–90)*

The case of the late-arriving student at Professor Galloway's lecture and Stephen Fry's reflections on his own time at university 30 years earlier could hardly offer a starker contrast in understandings about the role of lectures in higher education. They show how dramatically such attitudes have changed. Both involve students choosing whether to attend a lecture on the basis of seeking to decide if it represented something of value and interest to them. The student at New York University is widely condemned as acting in an irresponsible manner and 'like a customer' by shopping around. Another, more positive way of looking at the behavior of this student was that they were showing a strong sense of responsibility and personal engagement by simply trying to identify the course that suited them best.

By contrast, Stephen Fry argues that he did not find lectures particularly important in his own learning and preferred to read, talk with friends and attend the theater. He still managed to complete his course, receiving an upper second-class honors degree in English Literature, despite clearly attending very few lectures. While some might point to disciplinary differences in the value of lectures to learning, a point made by Stephen Fry in his own comments, there is something more fundamental here in thinking about how these two stories illustrate the way that the role of the student in higher education as a learner has come to be understood.

Conventionally, there has been a considerable emphasis on students at university taking responsibility for their own learning and becoming more independently minded. Going to university is often symbolically characterized as striking out on one's own. The highly structured and socially controlled environment of compulsory schooling has tended to contrast with life at uni-versity where students, particularly in the arts, social sciences and humanities, receive far less formal instruction on an average weekly basis than those studying laboratory-based subjects. All university students need to motivate themselves to study and manage their own time effectively. This is one of the timeless challenges of going to university and becoming an adult. Yet, attitudes appear to have shifted considerably if the quotations at the beginning of this chapter are any indication. Today's universities, and some of their professors, are becoming increasingly draconian in their attitude toward student attendance and 'engagement'. In a way this is paradoxical because higher education is ostensibly a voluntary activity for those who wish to learn beyond compulsory schooling. It is not a compulsory phase of education. As such, those that engage in higher education are normally, in most national contexts, considered to be adults able to exercise a free choice about how they spend their time and energy (see Chapter 2).

Why do student choose not to attend lectures? This is a brave question for institutions and individual professors to ask because the answers are not ones that they find easy to accept. One of the most common reasons that students give for missing a class is that they do not find it useful or value for time as they have too many other things to do (Dhimar, 2006; Harland et al., 2015). A survey of UK undergraduates found that more than half of those who skipped classes gave a lack of utility as the reason for their absence (HEPI, 2013: 11). This compared to just 10 percent of students citing work commitments for their absences. There are similarities here with the reason given by Stephen Fry for choosing to attend very few lectures when he was at university in the 1970s. He felt that he could use his time better in learning about English Literature by himself and in interacting with others. Fry believed that he learnt more informally – through reading, going to plays, discussion with others and so on – than formally by going to lectures. He not only believed he learnt better infor-mally, he was allowed to do so.

As Fry's narrative suggests, he may not necessarily have been working all the time. Yet in educational terms the description he gives of his activities suggests that he was mainly undertaking informal learning. This is something that has been defined as 'course-related activity undertaken individually and collabora-tively on campus that occurs outside the classroom' (Jamieson, 2009: 19). The role of informal or 'non-formal' learning has long been neglected in education but is said to account for the majority of learning in the workplace (Eraut, 2000: 113). It plays a very significant role in student learning at university and technology has added considerably to the opportunities for students to learn informally, independently and collaboratively with their peers beyond formal teaching sessions. The design of libraries and the learning resources provided at university has come to reflect the importance of informal spaces in student learning. Social network sites, such as Facebook, now play an important role (Vivian et al., 2014) along with the use of mobile devices within formal teaching sessions (Andrews and Jones, 2015) and anywhere the student happens to be at any time, on or off campus, in or out of class. Technological changes are blurring the boundary between formal and non-formal learning still further in all educational contexts.

Given the position of students as adult learners undertaking a voluntary activity, the advances in technology and the increasing importance and recognition of the role of informal or non-formal learning both at university and in the workplace it might seem a little odd that there is now so much emphasis placed on the importance of student attendance. The insistence that attendance is compulsory and always essential to learning flies in the face of this evidence as to why students are 'at' university and the multifarious ways in which they engage as learners. Nonetheless, such policies have increasingly come to characterize the treatment of university students as part of the creeping culture of performativity. This chapter will explore the way in which attendance policies are justified and how they demonstrate both a lack of trust in students and failure to respect their freedom to learn as an adult.

Presenteeism

A lot has changed in higher education since Stephen Fry was an undergraduate at Cambridge University in the 1970s. Absence from lectures or other classes is no longer tolerated as a matter of choice. Academics, and their universities, now tend to regard such behavior as unacceptable and a sign of a lack of so-called engagement, often blaming such absenteeism on student lifestyle choices. They see it as symptomatic of the pressures on young students to juggle busy lives and earn money to pay for their studies, as well as a failure to take these studies seriously enough. Sometimes they are less charitable in their reasoning and accuse students of being irresponsible or slovenly. The truth, that students do not attend classes because they do not find them particularly useful or stimulating, is the real, unpalatable reality that cuts into professional pride and the self-image of higher education institutions.

The case of the professor at New York University excluding a late-coming student is an indicator of the way that a culture of presenteeism has become a feature of higher education. Professor Galloway's own draconian policy of excluding anyone who turned up more than 15 minutes late is not unique or even particularly unusual. This is just one of a variety of punitive measures designed to enforce attendance that has produced a culture of presenteeism at university. Presenteeism is a term that is normally associated with the workplace rather than the university classroom. Yet much the same phenomenon can now be observed on university campuses. The term refers to employees who put in long working hours and feel impelled to attend work when ill or because of job insecurity or high work demands (Cooper, 1998; Caverley et al., 2007). As the antonym of absenteeism, presenteeism has attracted a good deal of interest from researchers in organizational behavior and human resource management studies. There has, though, been little consideration as to how students in higher education might be affected by this phenomenon except in relation to narrow definitions focusing exclusively on illness and depression (e.g. Law, 2007). Higher education students are further affected by presenteeism and the pressures on campus supporting the growth of this culture are growing. Universities are creating this culture through policies on attendance requirements, tasks that demand the presence of the student in order that they may be assessed during class contact time (such as in-class tests and oral presentations), rules on progression and high levels of assessment loading.

Attendance policies

Attendance policies are not a new phenomenon in higher education. What has changed in recent years, though, has been the manner in which they are now interpreted and enforced. Strict attendance rules are now common in higher education institutions enforced through a mix of institutional and departmental policies (e.g. Leufer and Cleary-Holdforth, 2010). Punitive measures, such as excluding late arriving students from class are evident (e.g. Middlesex University, 2011), as illustrated by Professor Galloway's personal policy. Some institutions, such as Goa University in India or University College London (UCL) in the UK, stipulate that students are not permitted to sit examinations unless they have met a minimum attendance threshold. At UCL, there is a minimum attendance requirement of 70 percent, although individual departments are free to stipulate a higher figure. A student who attends less often than this will be ineligible for summative assessment (UCL, 2015). Such a rule would have precluded Stephen Fry from taking his final examinations. Finally, advances in technology mean that electronic tracking systems have been introduced at a large number of universities (e.g. Bowen *et al.*, 2005). 'Swipe' cards record the presence of students in a classroom. Attendance data is gathered in a stealthy manner too via online learning platforms used by universities, such as Blackboard.

Justifications for compulsory attendance requirements essentially fall into three categories. These are a responsibility to be accountable to society which funds public higher education (*accountability argument*), a concern for student welfare that might be the cause of absence from class (*student well-being argument*) and to develop students with appropriate work-related attitudes and dispositions, such as punctuality and reliability (*work preparation argument*) (Macfarlane, 2013).

Accountability argument

The basis of the accountability argument is that it is a student's responsibility to attend class, given that they are in receipt of some form of public or private sponsorship in respect to their educational experience. The state subsidizes higher education through public investment while others, such as parents and some employers, act, in effect, as private investors who directly fund or subsidize places. While private and corporate higher education has grown in recent years, universities continue to be publicly funded. Despite the marketization of higher education, notably the creation of markets in students (Brown, 2013), the role of the state has become increasingly 'hands-on' given the growing importance of this sector for knowledge-based economies. The importation of management principles into the public sector means that the state is concerned to see universities offering an efficient return on investment. Hence, higher education is increasingly regarded as an economic investment made by a range of stakeholders, notably parents, employers, the government and wider society. According to this argument, a failure to attend on the part of students is an insupportable waste of public and private funding. On occasions, university attendance policies invoke this specific argument as the following example illustrates:

> The University recognizes the investment that students and their sponsors make when a student enrols on a course and believes that, as a responsible institution, it has a duty to monitor attendance and to act on non-attendance, so that students can be supported to complete their programs of study.
>
> (University of Bolton, 2011: 1)

Governments, and their respective funding agencies, are, so the argument goes, key stakeholders in higher education who are concerned about student non-completion as a waste of resources and as an indicator of inefficiency. This is why institutions need to report on, and are monitored in respect to, their completion and non-completion rates. Often higher education funding agencies in different national contexts will withhold funding from institutions until several months after the beginning of the academic year. This increases the incentive for institutions to keep a close eye on attendance in order to maximize their income stream from teaching activities. This in turn means that there is frequently an added financial incentive for universities to design means of improving student attendance as part of seeking to minimize non-completion.

The assumptions of accountability arguments are closely connected with the ideology of new managerialism (Deem and Brehony, 2005). Teaching-led institutions, heavily reliant on government funding for student places, are the ones most likely to respond to such pressures. Students graduating from these institutions are more liable to have lower social and cultural capital and tend to face potential labor market disadvantage. Hence, in this context, the motives of institutions in adopting a more directive approach toward attendance requirements may be viewed sympathetically as an attempt to maximize the chances of their students developing the skills needed to compete more effectively upon graduation.

Another justification for compulsory attendance policies on the basis of the accountability argument is that institutions are legally bound to comply with government immigration rules aimed at ensuring that international students are attending classes and abiding by their visa restrictions. In the UK, universities have a legal duty to report students from outside of the European Union with so-called 'tier 4' visas to the UK Border Agency (UKBA) when a student has missed ten consecutive working days or ten 'learning contacts' (e.g. Canterbury Christ Church University, 2010). The University of Leeds attendance monitoring policy states in its introduction that it is designed to 'provide a co-ordinated response to the UKBA's reporting requirements' (University of Leeds, 2011). Institutions who do not comply with UKBA reporting requirements risk deregistration and prosecution.

The final accountability argument is that it is important for students to attend class in order to demonstrate respect for peers and teachers as members of a learning community. The attendance policy of the University of Bolton in the UK states that late arrival or early departure from classes is 'unprofessional and unfair to other class members and tutors' (2011: 2), while that of the University of Leeds states that attendance is important because it 'fosters a culture of courtesy towards teaching staff and other students' (2011: 13). The policy issued by Heriot Watt University more directly emphasizes the importance of 'encouraging active participation through regular attendance in all areas of study' (2007: 1). Similar arguments can be found in the attendance policies of a large number of other universities. Here, the assertion is that attendance is critical in building up a sense of belonging to the group or cohort and of the importance of active and collaborative learning. This implies that students are in a communal sense accountable to both their peers and tutors. It is an argument that fits contemporary expectations that pedagogy should be focused more on the active engagement of students as learners rather than relying on a so-called didactic model of teaching. This argument can be invoked on the added basis that attendance is necessary given the emphasis now placed in university classrooms on active and collaborative approaches to learning. There is a strong moral undertone to this argument as it involves developing students with the right 'attitudes'. Non-attendance at class is identified as a matter of moral censure; a behavior that is indicative of a lack of respect for teachers and peers (University of Bolton, 2011; University of Leeds, 2011). This was clearly one of the criticisms leveled at the student who came late to Professor Galloway's class. His reaction indicates that he perceived the student's behavior as a personal affront.

Student well-being argument

A second way in which attendance policies are justified is on the basis of *student well-being*. According to one strand of this argument, universities should be concerned for the social, psychological and emotional welfare of students, and attendance is an important means by which they are able to fulfill this duty of care. This duty still exists even though in most international contexts the university is no longer acting *in loco parentis*. It is though, as noted in Chapter 3, held responsible for the physical, and to some extent emotional and psychological, health of its students. In recent years, institutions have established more professional support for students, such as counseling and financial advice services. Western society has developed greater openness about issues connected with psychological health and this is reflected in what has been somewhat disparagingly termed the 'anxious campus' (Vye *et al.*, 2007: 3), one which recognizes that students experience a range of psychological and emotional problems while at university. While personal tutoring by academics may be in decline due to massification and changing conceptions with respect to personal freedom and lifestyle choices (see Chapter 3), universities have developed a burgeoning infrastructure of professional support services to deal with social problems encountered by students.

Reflecting this trend, attendance policies invoke a language related to the importance of student support and guidance from a pastoral perspective. Heriot Watt University in Scotland states that their attendance policy 'has been developed as part of the University's commitment to provide a supportive learning environment' (Heriot Watt University, 2007: 1). Canterbury Christ Church University (2010: 3–7) has what it calls a 'cause for care and concern procedure', which involves a student being invited to discuss 'any problems' with their personal tutor. Here, the suggestion is that attendance requirements are necessary to monitor student well-being from a pastoral as well as academic point of view. Absence may be an indicator that a student is experiencing personal, social or financial problems and therefore it is important to find out whether any of these issues may be relevant. Appropriate action, according to policy statements, can then be taken to refer the student to support services depending on their individual needs. The University of Bolton details the responsibility of academic faculty for drawing the attention of student support services toward students who they feel might be 'at risk' (University of Bolton, 2011: 2). Here, the thinking is that being at university is only one element of a student's lifestyle, particularly for those who are in employment on either a part-time or full-time basis. It is recognized that students may feel isolated and lonely in mass higher education institutions and that monitoring attendance is a means of ensuring that teachers can 'keep an eye' on students and provide an early warning system in respect to their welfare needs.

A second strand of the student well-bring argument justifies attendance policies by linking this requirement to academic performance. Here it is contended that regular attendance leads to improved academic performance. At the core of most university attendance policies is the contention that poor attendance has a detrimental effect on student learning and achievement. Alternatively, the same point is made more positively by asserting that attendance leads to students achieving better grades. Students who do not attend are thus regarded as more likely to drop out of their studies, do less well in coursework and examinations, or simply fail. The attendance policy of Missouri State University states: 'Because class attendance and course grades are demonstrably and positively related, the university expects students to attend all class sessions of courses in which they are enrolled' (2012: 1).

There is a body of literature that broadly supports this contention, although the evidence is not overwhelming (Gendron and Pieper, 2005; Allen and Webber, 2010). In a study of business and economics students, attendance was found to have a small, but statistically significant, effect on their academic performance (Rogers, 2001). The possibility of teacher bias in giving students who attend more regularly a higher grade tends to undermine the strength of this contention. To some extent it could further be argued that the academic performance argument is really a sub-set of the stakeholder argument in that universities need to demonstrate good results to justify the public funding they receive.

Work preparation argument

Finally, arguments connected with preparation for the workplace emphasize that students need to attend, and develop dispositions such as punctuality, as these are expectations associated with future employment. Universities seek to justify attendance policies on the basis of student preparation for the workplace and in order that they can enter a variety of professions as competent and so-called safe practitioners. There are essentially two strands to this line of reasoning. First, it is said that students studying any program need to be familiarized with the expectations and demands of the workplace. In this respect, punctuality and reliable attendance are attitudes that students need to learn on any degree program. This is the 'real world' argument that, if students were employees, they would be expected to be punctual and would not have the choice as to whether or not to attend. The attendance policy of the University of Leeds (2011: 4) states that attendance is important because it 'helps students to build work patterns appropriate for their time after university'. These types of justifications are seen at course and unit level within business and management and teacher education programs.

Depending on the nature of the subject, it is sometimes further argued that students studying to enter a profession need to attend to ensure future competence or safe practice. Attendance is considered to be of heightened importance for students studying a variety of degree programs specifically linked to, or validated in conjunction with, professional bodies in medical-related occupations. Tensions can arise between professional and academic values in practice-based programs that draw on a wide variety of professorial expertise within an integrated framework, such as nursing (Leufer and Cleary-Holdforth, 2010). Here, 'covering' the curriculum is considered essential in order to be a safe and competent practitioner, particularly in professions where human lives can be at risk if students do not learn key knowledge and skills. Student non-attendance for theoretical instruction is a concern now more than ever for nurse educators as this may pose ramifications for the profession and indeed for public safety (Leufer and Cleary-Holdforth, 2010: section 18.3). A nurse being able to take an accurate blood pressure reading might be an example of why it is argued that attendance is essential to safe practice. The importance of regular attendance is further stressed in the context of certain other subjects, such as the learning of foreign languages, where absence might cause students to fall behind quickly and then be unable to catch up (University of Pennsylvania, 2012).

Attendance proxies

Compulsory attendance rules mean that *bodily performativity* is now an established part of the higher education experience of university students. There are, though, other more subtle ways in which the learning and teaching regime ensures that students attend class. These are attendance proxies. They can take a variety of different forms although the most common one is a class contribution grade. These are well established in a North American context (Bean and Peterson, 1998) but have more recently become common elsewhere in the Anglosphere. In a UK context, it is now not unusual for class attendance or contribution grades of between 5 percent and 10 percent to be awarded (Attwood, 2009). Although this may appear modest they can be closer to 20 percent (Ni Raghallaigh and Cunniffe, 2013). Most class contribution grades are, in effect, a grade for attendance rather than the evaluation of an individual student's actual contribution in class, making it a bodily rather than a participative performance. Ni Raghallaigh and Cunniffe (2013) justify their use of such a grade for attendance on the basis of continuity of group work and appropriate preparation for the course examination, based on the class contact sessions. This combines the assertion that attendance is some sort of moral responsibility, echoing the argument about respect for peers, combined with a dose of pragmatic self-interest.

Where student contribution in class is evaluated this often involves recording the number of times students get involved in activities or discussion. Graduate teaching assistants have traditionally been used in North America and can be employed to quantitatively record such information typically based on oral presentations or in posing and answering questions in whole class contexts (Long and Bedard, 1985). Here, the performative aspects of class contribution are stressed in formal assessment criteria at the expense of more subtle, but harder to measure and less demonstrative, aspects of non-verbal engagement such as active listening or note taking. Assessment rubrics, where they exist at all, tend to be very rudimentary and focus almost exclusively on visible aspects of student engagement. This is the classic problem with performative assessment that only seeks to measure the visible as opposed to the often more significant aspects of real performance and achievement, academic or otherwise.

There are a range of more subtle attendance proxies used in higher education to ensure that students come to class. In-class tests or short examinations undertaken in the classroom can be set on a regular basis at the beginning of a teaching session. Students failing to get to the class on time will fail the test. A more sophisticated version of this attendance proxy that demonstrates how little the student is trusted is to award a final grade on the basis of a student's best results from a small number of weekly tests. This rewards students with better attendance records by discounting their lower performing tests from certain weeks and builds in an incentive for students to attend all sessions punctually in order to get the chance to take all the tests and thereby maximize their possible grade. The assessment of oral presentations in class is another form of attendance proxy. If students fail to attend they may fail the assessment as well. A further type of attendance proxy is the withholding of lecture notes or other materials by teachers from students who have not attended a class. Sometimes such materials are withheld from online learning platforms for much the same reasons.

Assessment fatigue

Presenteeism is associated with occupations with high workplace and productivity demands. There is a direct parallel here with a higher education context where studies have shown that exhaustion among university students is extreme even in comparison with occupations customarily associated with high work demands. In a Canadian study, university students recorded a higher exhaustion level than 'high-exhaustion' occupations such as social work, teaching and public accountancy (Law, 2007). Exhaustion is often associated with the over-assessment of university students squeezing out time for other activities (Ditcher, 2001). One of the reasons for the increasing work demands faced by students is modularization allied to over-assessment. Modularization is widely acknowledged to have led to expansion in the volume of assessment (Bloxham and Boyd, 2007). Assessment fatigue amongst students has been further exacerbated by the adoption of outcomes-based assessment leading to a concern to 'cover' all learning outcomes. This has increased the number of assessments.

A study at a university in New Zealand provides important insights into why students do not attend lectures (Harland et al., 2015). The study shows that assessment workload is a key reason why students missed teaching sessions. The frequency of grading within relatively short modules meant that students needed to direct their effort at these tasks in order to successfully progress. Such systems of learning and assessment, whereby students gain credits on the basis of a short module and multiple assessments, is common across higher education. The reality, as revealed in the study by Harland and his colleagues, is that students are required to complete between 0.68 and 1.44 graded assessments *per week* (Harland et al., 2015). It is hardly surprising that this exhausting assessment regime means that students are impelled to prioritize work on assignments rather than attend lectures and other classes.

When students fail to attend classes at university it is common to blame them for disrespectful attitudes and a consumerist mentality, but it is important to understand the underlying reasons why students do not turn up. At the beginning of this chapter it was noted that the most common reason students give for missing a class is that they do not find it useful. There is a tendency to blame non-attendance on the fact that students are working and have busy lives, but in a survey of UK undergraduates over half who skipped classes explained that the reason for their absence was that the teaching lacked utility (HEPI, 2013: 11). This was the most common reason given compared to just 10 percent of students who cited work commitments.

Further evidence of the reasons underlying student non-attendance are provided by Dhimar (2006) in a study of student non-attendance at a UK university.

This study identifies illness, social life and the demands of, or catching up with, academic work as the top three reasons cited. Employment was the second lowest rated of the reasons given by students. A much more common explanation for missing sessions was dislike of the teaching approach, mentioned by more than one-fifth of the sample, or as part of a course, mentioned by 38 percent of those questioned. In asking students about their views on individual courses (or 'modules'), a number of comments betray their dissatisfaction with the use of group work assessment as an attendance proxy:

> despite module not being liked, attendance was high because of compulsory assessment component of group work assignment.
>
> (Dhimar, 2006: 25)

> 50% group presentation (weighting was felt to be too high).
>
> (Dhimar, 2006: 27)

A number of other studies have pointed to the importance of good quality teaching in determining whether students decide to attend or not (Kelly, 2012; Dolnicar, 2005; Dolnicar *et al.*, 2009; Friedman *et al.*, 2001). The way that students define teaching quality does not necessarily coincide with how academics define it. Here there has been a neglect of the importance of perceptions of value for time and whether a lecture is considered to sufficiently 'cover' the ground. Those committed to active learning approaches dismiss such considerations as evidence of surface learning. Yet, clearly students may evaluate a class negatively if it means that they do not feel that it has offered them value for time.

Teaching that is considered poor value for time and over-assessment are important reasons why students do not wish to attend classes. Although a common justification for regular coursework assessment is that this helps to motivate students, it is used 'as a deterrent to reduce the frequency of unwanted behaviours' and 'destroys any intrinsic motivation or willingness to take risks essential to learner autonomy' (Wass *et al.*, 2015: 1325). Even though educators want students to undertake deep learning the demands of the curriculum provide them in reality with little opportunity to do so. Advocates of deep learning blame students who do not approach their studies in this way for acting in an instrumental manner by adopting a strategic approach. Yet, students are only acting this way because of the conditions created for them by the higher education system, the institutions and the academics that teach within it. Part of the problem here is the way that modularization has fragmented academic knowledge into smaller and smaller chunks and placed students under pressure to complete coursework at the expense of any opportunity to engage more deeply in understanding the subject. So, while some students may be 'only working for a grade' (Harland *et al.*, 2015: 534), this is largely the product of over-assessment within a modularized system of learning and teaching. Students are simply being behaviorally conditioned by the assessment regime to act in this manner.

Conclusion

Attendance requirements are, to some extent, symptomatic of a crisis of confidence about the value of a higher education and a concern to demonstrate its so-called value to governments and parents as part of a performative culture. The literature is dominated by justifications based on claims that attendance improves student learning and completion rates (e.g. Bowen *et al.*, 2005). While some institutional policies provide justifications for rules on attendance, a large number provide no reasons whatsoever and baldly state procedures and penalties for non-compliance. The policy of UK and US universities in this area rarely, if ever, acknowledges the counter-argument that a compulsory attendance requirement is inappropriate in the context of a higher education that should respect a student's freedom to choose how to best utilize their study time, a principle that can be drawn from the work of Carl Rogers.

Most of the arguments made in support of compulsory attendance at university do not stand up to serious scrutiny. One of these is that students need to attend in order to meet the demands of safe practice in professional programs. However, bodily attendance does not, in itself, guarantee that an individual can successfully operationalize a skill or apply knowledge. This is the role of assessment, not attendance. All attendance guarantees is that the student was in the room at the time. Such an argument relies, perhaps unwittingly, on teacher-centered assumptions about how students learn. Neither does bodily performativity, nor just turning up at class, mean that students are actually engaging. Attendance should not be confused with *real*, authentic engagement. A student who attends a class may choose not to engage for any number of reasons, such as a lack of concentration, boredom, tiredness or a failure on the part of the teacher to communicate ideas effectively. On the other hand, someone who does not attend the formal class, may, through informal learning via reading, reflection, use of online resources or subsequent communication with peers, engage much more meaningfully and deeply.

Presenteeism is strangely at odds with the rhetoric of independent and lifelong learning. The demands of the contemporary workplace make adaptation and continuous professional development a necessity. The way in which we can learn has never been more flexible: the world wide web, social networking and connected mobile devices on the move. The physical 'classroom', be it a lecture theater, seminar room or laboratory, is part of a broader landscape of learning. Students learn in the workplace as well as on campus. Yet, university policies, and the prevailing assumptions of those that write them, are that students are young and immature and incapable of managing their workload and personal lives. This means that they must attend all their classes in order to properly 'engage'. Students are further subject to assessment regimes that do the exact opposite of what they are intended to do: they de-motivate rather than motivate students and make them less rather than more autonomous as learners.

Chapter 7

Emotional performativity

The 'forced reflection'

As an undergraduate Valerie Hobbs took a course entitled 'Self in Society'. Her professor explained that he wanted the students in the class to write a number of 'reflective essays', the purpose of which was 'to encourage us to examine negative patterns of behavior in our families, like loosely veiled racism or gender stereotyping and thus become "agents of change" in our generation' (Hobbs, 2007: 405). Valerie Hobbs had reservations, though, about undertaking such an assignment having had no previous experience of writing a 'reflective essay'. She was also reluctant to reveal what she regarded as private and personal matters to someone she had only just met and hardly knew. Perhaps unsurprisingly she received a poor grade for her first reflective essay, in common with most other members of her class. The professor conveyed his dissatisfaction that the essays were insufficiently reflective. Valerie, along with her classmates, was unskilled, and perhaps unwilling, to be as frank about her personal feelings as the professor seemed to require.

Subsequently, though, Valerie undertook what she termed 'a strategic deception' (Hobbs, 2007: 414) by inventing what she regarded as relatively innocuous stories about sibling rivalry and disharmony in her family. By writing about this in her reflective essay she was able to maintain the privacy of her real family life and satisfy the demands of the assignment. As a result of this strategic deception her grades improved. Even though, in reality, her work was a fabrication of the truth her inventive reflections clearly had sufficient verisimilitude to be thought of as real. She felt she had met her professor's expectations. As she explained: 'Rather than a process towards self-development, this assignment became merely an exercise in perfecting my ability to anticipate what the professor wanted and to give it to him' (Hobbs, 2007: 414).

This personal story of how one student felt about being required to write a 'reflective essay', and how she managed to navigate this requirement, is illustrative of the changing nature of what it means to be a student in higher education. Writing about this experience later after becoming an academic herself, Valerie Hobbs describes it as a 'forced reflection' (Hobbs, 2007: 405). Such an assignment placed her, and the other students in the class, under a pressure of self-disclosure.

They were required to reveal their innermost thoughts and feelings in a kind of surveillance of their emotional and moral health.

The growing popularity of reflection and reflective practice in university assessment practice is part of a shift from knowing to becoming, from an understanding of higher education as an acquisition of knowledge and skills to the display of certain attitudes and values which fit notions of the contemporary citizen. It is an ontological turn and a clearly therapeutic one premised on the idea that confession is somehow good for the soul. How, it might be asked, has requiring students to reveal such private matters become not merely acceptable but widely regarded as good practice in higher education today? The answer is that self-confessional reflections such as the one produced by Valerie Hobbs are just one element of the wider phenomenon of emotional performativity.

In this chapter I will focus on two prominent examples of emotional performativity in higher education: global citizenship and self-reflection. The first requires students to give an emotional performance about *what they care about*, while the latter is concerned with students being required to provide evidence about *how they feel*. The former refers to and can be found prominently in the undergraduate curriculum while the latter is principally associated with postgraduate professional and doctoral education.

Global citizenship: showing that you care

If you visit a university website you will often be confronted by a strapline to the effect that the institution is producing 'good global citizens' or 'leaders for the 21st century' (Astin, 2002). Students, it is claimed, are being transformed as a result of their studies into 'global citizens' or 'reflective professionals'. In short, increasing numbers of higher education institutions across the world now see the development of students for 'active global citizenship' as a legitimate strategic aim (Bourn *et al.*, 2006: 1). The global citizenship agenda is enacted within the university curriculum in various ways through community and service learning programs, placements with charities and other non-governmental organizations, study abroad programs, electives or general education courses in four-year undergraduate degrees and via cross-curricular themes within a student's major. There are even stand-alone qualifications such as certificates and diplomas in Global Citizenship. Study abroad, service learning and collaborative learning have been identified as signature pedagogies of global citizenship in parallel with the use of moots and case studies in legal education (Brigham, 2011). Institutions around the world, such as University College London and the University of Bournemouth in the UK, the University of Sydney in Australia and the University of Hong Kong, have incorporated statements with respect to global citizenship within their overarching educational aims and expectations for student learning outcomes. Student societies and language immersion courses are sometimes included under the umbrella of global citizenship in an attempt to demonstrate the broader dedication to the values that are implied by this phrase.

The values encompassed by the phrase 'global citizenship' tend to incorporate an understanding and a celebration of difference in society. This typically includes a respect for other cultures, ethnicities and religions; a commitment to ethical and social responsibility in connection with environmental sustainability or campaigning to eliminate world poverty; and a willingness to offer leadership in a variety of settings, such as the community or in the workplace, to effect changes which accord with this agenda centered on global justice and social change. The notion of leadership for global citizenship is strongly related to bringing about change in future roles that graduates may occupy. This is seen as a way of taking the values and the goals of global citizenship forward into the future. The University of Alberta's Global Education program, for instance, 'inspires and cultivates students as the next generation of leaders prepared to tackle critical issues facing the globe' (University of Alberta, 2014). This statement typifies the strong transformational vision that lies behind attempts to foster global citizenship in educational settings, in both schools and universities.

Universities have long laid claim to the moral development of their students although this has previously been mainly centered on the religious roots of many institutions. Until the late nineteenth century, English universities applied a religious test to exclude Catholics or others who chose not to swear allegiance to the Church of England. Religious tests were abolished in 1871 but religion, together with new, more broadly inclusive definitions of spirituality, has continued to play a prominent role in most national systems of higher education. The concept of spirituality has fed into the contemporary focus on global citizenship. Astin and colleagues (2011: 20–21) argue that spiritual growth and spirituality are fundamental to a university education. In defining what they mean by spirituality the authors identify ten measures of spirituality and religiousness. While these include fairly conventional 'measures of religiousness' such as religious commitment to particular faiths and religious engagement though activities such as praying, they comprise 'measures of spirituality'. Within this category spiritual quest is defined as 'searching for meaning/purpose in life, finding answers to the mysteries of life, attaining an inner harmony, and developing a meaningful philosophy of life' (Astin *et al.*, 2011: 20–21). These authors further identify equanimity as the second of these two 'internally' focused elements of spirituality. This is defined as feeling at peace or being 'centered', and three further 'externally' oriented measures: the ethic of caring, charitable involvement and what is described as an ecumenical worldview. This set of values is closely connected with a view of global citizenship as a form of cosmopolitan citizenship. It is seen as an exemplar of an ethic of caring. The set of beliefs represented by world or global citizenship in this tradition include 'identification with all other human being as equals; belief that we share the earth in common; and commitment to peace and to tolerance of other religions and cultures' (Carter, 2001: 11). Sometimes this set of beliefs is encapsulated by the use of the term humanitarianism.

Global citizenship emerged, to some extent, in the early 1990s on the basis of increased international co-operation in the post-Cold War era that led to an increased emphasis on international agreements in respect to common global issues such as climate change. New communications technology and common threats to the human race, such as environmental degradation and nuclear weapons, are other important factors in stimulating interest in global citizenship (Carter, 2001). However, citizenship is a normative and ideologically charged concept based on a multitude of competing explanations and claims. It is not a singular, non-political concept based on social consensus. According to Carter (2001), there is not one but two alternative models of citizenship. Republican ideas of citizenship focus on the importance of national defense against foreign attack in the spirit of the political social contract. Preventing conflicts between warring nation states has conventionally been a driving force in the development of international law. This republican view of citizenship is more concerned about responsibilities toward the nation state and may be traced back to the work of Thomas Hobbes, among other political theorists. Liberal ideas related to citizenship, by contrast, place more emphasis on individual citizens as bearers of certain rights, such as property ownership, and being able to hold their government to account through a social contract. The emergence of global markets for goods and services is seen within the liberal tradition as a benefit of globalization in lowering prices for the majority of people. Neo-liberal economists, such as Milton Friedman, have advocated the view that open markets ultimately provide the greatest benefits. In this tradition, the primary 'global responsibility' of a government is to promote free trade between nations. The emphasis here, on individualism as an expression of free trade, is at odds with a more collaborative version of global citizenship based on a primary concern for social justice rather than a level playing field for the international exchange of goods and services.

In similar vein, Steger (2009) shows that there are different 'globalisms' stretching from the political right to the political left. On the right, market globalism interprets the forces of globalization as evidence of the pre-eminence of neo-liberal forces such as free trade, privatization and the weakness of the nation state to control the boundaries of commerce. On the political left, a different interpretation of globalization prevails which Steger (2009) refers to as justice globalism. This stresses a social justice agenda that can only be achieved through global co-operation and encompasses the elimination of poverty, more equitable income distribution, international human rights and the protection of the environment. The Clinton Global Citizen Awards, established in 2007 by the former US president, is symbolic of the importance attached to action-oriented social change valued by those allied to this position. The values of justice globalism center on collectivism and social activism whereas market globalism is about laissez-faire neo-liberal individualism.

The phrase 'global citizenship' is widely invoked in both school and university contexts and understandings of globalism relate directly to the way this phrase is interpreted. When questioned, student understanding of global citizenship appears to squarely align with the claims of justice globalism. In a study of Canadian student perspectives about global citizenship, inequality was identified as the most common concern along with other issues connected with justice globalism such as poverty, gender inequity, sustainability, the environment and human rights (Roddick, 2007). The dominance of justice globalism in student understandings of this phrase are hardly surprising given the long history and influence of service learning, education for action and other community engagement projects on university campuses. Student perspectives are further shaped by the growth of citizenship education in schools over the last 20 years. Citizenship education has been a growth area internationally since the 1980s and has been a statutory subject in the UK school national curriculum since 2002. Oxfam, among other leading charities, has established support for 'active' global citizenship providing learning materials for schools, aimed at making the world 'a more just and sustainable place' (Oxfam, 2013).

Universities interpret globalism in terms of a social justice and action-oriented agenda. In Steger's (2009) terms this interpretation falls comfortably within the justice globalism camp. This orientation is evidenced in the university curriculum and through extra-mural activities on an international basis often within university general education and elective programs. In Canada, the World University Service of Canada (WUSC) supports what is termed a 'Global Citizens for Change' initiative while in the UK and Australia universities have developed sets of graduate attributes which contain explicit expectations that students will become advocates of global citizenship (Barrie, 2004; Cousin et al., 2013). At the University of Sydney global citizenship is one of three 'holistic, overarching attributes' (Barrie, 2004: 271) expected of undergraduate students along with scholarship and lifelong learning. A similar emphasis on global citizenship can be found at other Australian universities such as Melbourne and Deakin. Influenced by Australian universities, global citizenship is one of several graduate attributes identified across Scottish universities and has been encouraged by the Quality Assurance Agency for Higher Education in Scotland as part of a curriculum enhancement project (Hounsell, 2011). Some universities, such as Bath Spa in the UK, even have a certificate in global citizenship for undergraduate students. At the University of Hong Kong, one of the four goals of the common core curriculum is to 'enable students to see themselves as members of global as well as local communities and to play an active role as responsible individuals and citizens in these communities' (University of Hong Kong, 2012: n.p.). Similar statements about curriculum intentions can be found at a large number of other universities. The way in which the higher education curriculum provides for such objectives is increasingly apparent in courses across a range of subjects and reflects the concerns of those who take a social justice perspective, leading to a focus on topics such as poverty, diversity and equality, sustainability and environmental degradation, as well as the effects of violence and conflict (Bourn et al., 2006). The emphasis on action and volunteering found in university statements on global citizenship is connected with the importance attached to student advocacy in promoting goals such as tackling world poverty and improving understanding across cultures. Hence, global citizenship has become a universal ethos that, while purporting to tackle difference and diversity, has also led to 'the domestication of difference' within a framework of Western liberal individualism (Dill, 2013: 98).

Casting to one side for a moment a certain degree of marketing hyperbole which institutional statements about global citizenship often represent, they indicate the extent to which universities now ascribe to themselves a role as molders or shapers of student belief systems. Universities have always been places that have asserted such a role but not, I would argue, in quite the same way in which this is now being expressed within the curriculum. To borrow a phrase from Rose (1990), this is about an attempt to govern the soul placing a requirement on students to give an emotional performance consistent with the attitudes and values sanctified by the university. This curriculum is as much about demonstrating an adherence to a set of normative beliefs as about engaging students in learning. It predetermines the beliefs that students are required to demonstrate about the world rather than allowing them choice in the matter on the basis of their own values and understanding of the issues. As such, it is about being required to sign up for a particular view of the way in which the world should be improved, 'changed', or 'transformed'. It requires students to give an *emotional performance* that fails to respect their freedom to learn.

Self-reflection: showing how you feel

In 1997, in the wake of the sudden death of Diana, Princess of Wales in a road accident in Paris, the Queen came in for sustained criticism from the British press and some members of the public. The criticism centered on the perceived failure of the Queen, and other members of the British royal family, to offer an immediate public display of their sorrow at Diana's death by returning to London from their country retreat in Scotland. Suggestions were made that the failure of the Queen to return from Scotland and appear in public showed she was cold and heartless. The tabloid press led demands that the Queen should return to London with headlines such as 'Has the House of Windsor a heart?' (*Daily Mail*) and 'Show us you care' (*Daily Express*). As a result of the criticism the Queen later made a television broadcast in which she paid personal tribute to Diana. The criticism died down but Diana's funeral was marked by an emotional display of public mourning rarely, if ever, seen in Britain before.

The criticism of the Queen in the wake of the death of the Princess of Wales is a frequently cited illustration of the way in which values have changed within British society, although the extent to which this one event was significant is highly disputed within the academic literature. It is agreed, though, that while grief used to be understood as a purely private matter the mores of society have noticeably shifted toward what is termed 'expressive grief' (Walter, 1999: 148) or 'expressive individualism' (Bellah *et al.*, 1985). This appears to indicate that new performative norms are emerging in Western society in relation to grief and in the conduct of funerals. Part of this is a growing acceptance of an expressivist perspective that letting emotions out publicly rather than keeping them bottled up in private is better for the psychological health of the bereaved.

Showing how you feel is now part of a much wider trend toward what Fejes and Dahlstedt (2013) call a 'confessing society' (see Chapter 3). Confession is now considered good for the soul and this way of thinking has infiltrated the university classroom in a number of ways. Personal writing assignments have a long history in American higher education dating back to the late nineteenth century and are particularly associated with literature and composition classes. This has been labeled 'risky writing' (Berman, 2001) since it involves self-disclosure and shame as part of a process of reflecting on experiences. The two are interconnected in this genre since 'the more one self-discloses, the greater the threat of shame' (Berman, 2001: 22). The emotional dimension is now very much in the mainstream. The considerable influence and popularity of Goleman's (1995) work on emotional intelligence, and the way this has been adapted and adopted in the context of learning and teaching in higher education, needs to be understood as part of the way that disclosing the personal is now seen as part of what is expected of university students. The professor is expected to be not just knowledgeable, but emotionally intelligent too, in the way that they go about teaching students (Mortiboys, 2002).

In the contemporary higher education classroom, it is not only students of literature and creative writing who are encouraged to undertake 'risky writing' by getting personal when writing an assignment. This now applies to students across several subjects where expressive forms of writing containing confession and self-disclosure are a standard part of self-reflection and reflective practice exercises. For some years now, prompted in part by the work of Schön, Dewey, Habermas and Kolb (Ross, 2011), self-reflection has been strongly connected with action-oriented professions such as architecture, nursing, social work and teaching. Here, reflective writing practices are seen as a helpful means by which trainee professionals can connect theoretical knowledge with the reality of practice. Self-reflection, as part of experiential learning, is used widely in the university curriculum as a basis for getting students to consider how their values and attitudes have impacted on, and perhaps been reshaped by, their learning in practice settings.

There are a number of types of self-reflection commonly used within higher education at both undergraduate and postgraduate level and particularly, though not exclusively, associated with professional and practice-based degree programs in areas such as nursing, teaching, social work, engineering and even accountancy. The reason for the use of self-reflection assignments and expectations within other forms of assessment may be largely attributed to a widespread belief that reflection is an aid to the enhancement of learning and, in particular, where theoretical knowledge is applied in practice. Self-reflection is meant to provide an authentic insight into the way a student's thinking has been shaped, and perhaps reshaped by certain experiences.

There are various names given to self-reflection type assessments at university – reflective diaries, learning logs, journals and (e-)portfolios, among others. Some are intended as a vehicle for showing how students in professional or practice-based areas have thought about what they have done in their practice or work placements, sometimes referred to as reflection-on-action (Schön, 1991). This means that students are expected to reflect on how successful they have been or what they have learnt from an activity after it has occurred, such as a work placement or, indeed, any encounter in a practice-based setting such as a business organization, hospital or clinic. Self-reflections, though, may be used with students on any course as a way of asking them to think about their feelings and responses to any issue (e.g. racism) without any necessary link to professional learning. This applies as much to a student of, say, history as engineering.

Self-reflective exercises play an important role in portfolios or e-portfolios. These are a collection of artefacts and documents evidencing learning and meeting of learning outcomes, often exemplifying some form of professional practice as well as containing a reflection element. Reflection is an important part of a portfolio or e-portfolio. At the course level the purpose of an e-portfolio is to both 'document and reflect' (Stefani et al., 2007: 11). Here, reflection refers to the evaluation of learning growth over time including understanding what has and has not been achieved (Stefani et al., 2007: 19). The reflection is so ubiquitous that almost nine out of ten teacher preparation programs in the US use portfolios as one form of assessment of their students (Salzman et al., 2002).

Self-reflective exercises are based on the philosophy of experiential learning which itself is a 'process whereby people . . . engage in direct encounter, then *purposefully* reflect upon, validate, transform, give personal meaning to and seek to integrate their different ways of knowing' (McGill and Warner Weil, 1989: 248). The word transform is significant here in defining experiential learning since it denotes an expectation that a self-reflective exercise will evidence some kind of personal epiphany. This is why an 'emotionally disturbing experience' or a 'critical incident' (Moon, 2004: 4, 166), taking place in work-based or personal life settings, are often seen as central to reflective learning.

Experiential and service learning are pedagogies closely associated with promoting the goals of global citizenship through the use of both reflective journals and observations. They take a variety of forms and often involve working in the community with voluntary and other non-profit organizations or in response to local needs or problems. An example is provided by a community service project undertaken by students from the University of Hong Kong in a post-earthquake area in the Sichuan region of mainland China in 2009. The project was designed as a way for students to develop various graduate attributes including 'leadership skills, global citizenship and cultural understanding' (Chan, 2012: 414). It involved students from engineering, education and computing in helping to reconstruct a primary school. Students were assessed via their 'reflective observations' (p. 414) designed to demonstrate how they had connected theory with practice and gained new insights. Part of the purpose of such learning is in the way it 'connects students' emotions and empathy towards the subject matter' (Chan, 2012: 413).

Hence, self-reflective assignments place considerable emphasis on students revealing how new knowledge gained from practice can be supplantive as well as additive and, therefore, emotionally disturbing in disrupting previously held beliefs. Given that cognition is a supplantive as well as an additive process, teachers in higher education, especially those influenced by ideas about experiential learning, are interested in seeing how such transformations in thinking are occurring via reflective learning exercises. The self-reflective exercise has thus become a channel through which students are expected to show their thinking has changed or been 'transformed'. The marshalling of the emotions as a component of academic writing is central to the art of reflection evidenced by the numerous references to 'emotional processes' and 'emotional insight' which appear in the index for the *Handbook of Reflective and Experiential Learning* written by Jenny Moon, a leading proponent of self-reflection in higher education.

Incorporating self-reflection into the university curriculum threatens a student's personal privacy. Students are expected to divulge information of a personal and private nature that not all may wish to share with others. A diary or journal is, by definition, a highly personal and private document, something that is not associated with being available for others to scrutinize and, ultimately, grade. Those who promote the use of reflective diaries or journals like to emphasize the freedom they give students to record their thoughts, feelings and reflections on actions unbounded by the usual, restrictive academic conventions. Wood (2013) quotes approvingly from Rainer's (1978) book *The New Diary*:

> The diary is the only form of writing that encourages total freedom of expression. Because of its very private nature, it has remained immune from any formal rules of content, structure or style. As a result the diary has come closest to reproducing how people really think and how consciousness evolves.
> (Rainer, 1978: 11)

The reality for students could not be further from the truth when considering the way in which such self-reflective journals are actually used in the higher education curriculum. They may be intended to give 'freedom of expression' but there are tacit rules that determine their content, structure and style when used and assessed in an academic context. Such rules may be absent from genuinely private and personal journals kept by individuals with a desire to do so, but are clearly apparent in self-reflection forms of assessment in higher education. Here, assessment rubrics often suggest that it is better to write in the first person singular as a way of conveying the sense of the deeply personal. Publications on self-reflection in higher education make it clear that what is being looked for from the student is to demonstrate transformational stories and effects result-ing from reflections-on-action or reflections-on-life experiences. Jane Wood's *Transformation through Journal Writing* (2013) is a case in point. Even the book title demonstrates the intent of what is being sought.

There is a great deal of pious advice about the importance of protecting the identity of others in the writing of self-reflective assignments. These might be workplace colleagues, patients or clients, or perhaps family members or friends. Using aliases is recommended rather than revealing their identity as this would compromise their privacy. Yet, it seems not to occur to those that advocate self-reflection that the students asked to complete such exercises may not necessarily wish to make revealing statements about their own values and attitudes. Wood admits that some students dislike reflective diaries and see them as 'an invasion of privacy' (Wood, 2013: 5). Some students are more likely to be 'low disclos-ers' (Berman, 2001) who do not wish to reveal personal values and emotional reactions, perhaps because they wish to protect their privacy. This is a common concern expressed by students in research studies about the use of self-reflection. In one such study students expressed anxiety that 'if they attempted any degree of honesty in the assignment they felt it made them very vulnerable' (Stewart and Richardson, 2000: 373). It is, perhaps, hardly surprising that some students, or indeed any person, might be reluctant to reveal their innermost thoughts, feel-ings and emotions to someone they hardly know. Counseling and psychotherapy relationships are based on informed consent and strict confidentiality. Seeking to apply the former type of relationship to student learning in higher education without the latter is clearly problematic.

The fact that some students are disinclined to enter into genuine disclosure can lead to them adopting strategies to protect their privacy in a similar manner to that described by Valerie Hobbs at the beginning of this chapter. The reality is that tutors cannot be sure whether a student's self-reflection is real or simply invented to give the desired effect (Nesi, 2008). For a generation that has grown up in the world of social networking the protection of personal privacy through the invention of alternative identities is a familiar means of self-protection. Even enthusiastic advocates of self-reflection admit that detecting inauthenticity is one of the problems of marking these types of assignments. Yet, the fact that higher education teachers think it is legitimate to police for levels of sincerity demonstrates the embedded nature of emotional performativity.

Whether self-reflection should be graded or not is a contentious issue within the literature, with some researchers arguing that it is either very difficult to assess (e.g. Morrison, 1996) or better not to assess at all given the way in which this might inhibit students from being truthful about what they do not know as well as what they do know (e.g. Sumsion and Fleet, 1996; Boud, 2001). Evidence suggests that non-native speakers of English and students from cer-tain cultural contexts may be disadvantaged when trying to write in a reflective genre (Clarkeburn and Kettula, 2012). The grading of self-reflective assign-ments may be perceived by a student as a judgment about them as a person as opposed to a grade for an academic piece of work. Students may further believe that being skillful in the right reflective writing genre will get them a better grade. Yet, the reality is that self-reflective assignments are very often assessed despite the ambiguous or uncertain nature of what is being judged, which both students and staff often find difficult to understand (Stewart and Richardson, 2000).

It is not just undergraduate or taught postgraduate students who are now required to demonstrate their emotional performativity via self-reflection. The growing popularity of auto-ethnography research is symbolic of the way in which the self is increasingly seen as a mainstream subject of investigation. As academics embrace such methods the heightened stress placed on demonstrating emotional performativity applies increasingly to research students. Research postgraduate students are required to complete a dissertation, thesis or research report, of varying length depending on the academic level of their program. Within these extended pieces of academic writing students are expected to justify their methodological approach, frequently through a stand-alone chapter. At doctoral level this is a common feature of a written thesis. Conventionally, a methodology chapter might consist of a discussion of alternative research paradigms and an explanation and justification for the approach chosen in addressing the research question or problem. It is within this context that there has been a growing emphasis on students developing 'positionality' statements intended to explore and explain the relationship between the researcher and the research topic. Here, the idea is that a researcher's positionality consists of their personal beliefs, values, political outlook, assumptions and prejudices. Within the social sciences, there is a belief that:

> a researcher's social, cultural and subject positions (and other psychological processes) affect: the questions they ask; how they frame them; the theories that they are drawn to; how they read; their relations with those they research in the field or through interviews; interpretations they place on empirical evidence; access to data, institutions and other outlets for research dissemination; and the likelihood that they will be listened to and heard.
>
> (Gregory *et al.*, 2011: 556)

This implies a need for a reflexive self-awareness about how someone's social identity impacts on the choices they make as a researcher. It is an all-encompassing concept related to the self and self-awareness. In many respects the idea of a positionality statement is well grounded since all researchers need to clarify their assumptions and beliefs, understand how these might be related to personal values, and thereby identify methods that are congruent with their own research philosophy. This is a stricture that might apply as much to those conducting quantitative research in the hard sciences as qualitative research in the humanities or social sciences, although researcher positionality statements are more readily connected with the latter.

The writing of positionality statements by research students makes similar demands to other forms of self-reflective writing for confession, apology and a large dose of self-justification. It encourages what Cousin (2010: 9) has described as 'positional piety' whereby 'either moral authority is claimed through an affinity with subjects (such as working-class woman) or through a confessional dec-laration of difference and relative privilege (such as white middle-class man)'. Possessing either the right 'class positionality' or 'colored positionality' gives the researcher a privileged sense of their own entitlement and insight into the sub-jects of their study (Cousin, 2010: 10, 11). By contrast, anyone with the temerity to think they can research a social group of which they are not already a member is required to enter into a detailed apology for their social identity, particularly if they hail from an overly privileged class. Like all self-reflective statements, this risks that they can take on an almost ritualistic quality leading to ultimate self-affirmation through confession.

Conclusion

Service learning via global citizenship and the use of self-reflection through work-based and experiential learning are relatively recent additions to the uni-versity curriculum that require emotional performativity from students. They are a further illustration of self-commodification in that students need to demon-strate their emotions in relation to their own learning and the way in which they empathize with others, along with issues of justice globalism, such as poverty and inequality. The effect of the promotion of such values, as with other elements of emotional performativity, needs to be understood in the context of research which has shown that shyness, a lack of preparation for discussion and fear of contradicting the views of the professor can lead students to self-censor when asked to discuss value-based concepts such as multiculturalism (Hyde and Ruth, 2002). Rather than appear uncaring or selfish students must give an emotional performance to demonstrate their commitment to experiential learning, global citizenship, sustainable development, lifelong learning or any number of other normative mantras. This runs the very real risk of turning learning at university into a form of political correctness. Learning needs to be about authenticity, not compliance. Most crucially, in the words of Carl Rogers, it threatens student freedom to learn 'without pressure' (Rogers, 1951: 395). Students should be free to learn without the requirement that they need to demonstrate emotional compliance with politically fashionable ideas or theories. Real freedom allows students to make up their own minds on the basis of focusing on evaluating the veracity of knowledge claims.

Chapter 8

Reclaiming student-centered

Introduction

The argument I have sought to construct in this book is that there is a need to reclaim the concept of student-centered. For too long this phrase has been narrowly interpreted as about providing opportunities for student participation in class and learning actively rather than passively. As I have contended, student-centeredness is based on an understanding that higher education is a process of emancipation rather than one of constraint and control imposed by a creeping culture of student performativity. To be truly student-centered requires an empathetic understanding of what it means to be a learner and a respect for the ideas of freedom and democracy. This is about allowing real student choice, as opposed to a superficial one that is based on selecting from a variety of modules that offer the same diet of compulsory attendance requirements, participative and emotional performativity and over-assessment. To be genuinely student-centered it is necessary to recognize that studying at university is, almost by definition, a voluntary activity entered into by autonomous adults.

Unfortunately, student engagement at university has become a mantra that has hijacked the concept of student-centered as a means of justifying the rituals of performativity, now widespread across higher education. Student engagement is based on a false set of assumptions about what needs to be measured (e.g. time and effort) and fails to respect the maturity of the learner and their right to make choices about what, when and how to learn. Students should be free to choose how they wish to learn and to participate in higher education in ways in which *they* see as valuable. This is what being student-centered is about. It is not about surveillance or legislating a one-size-fits-all approach making compulsory attendance or active participation a must in class.

In this concluding chapter I will argue that it is possible to reclaim a genuinely student-centered higher education if we do a number of things. First, we need to place a renewed emphasis on the importance of independent learning, allowing students to make more choices about their curriculum and the nature of their engagement at university. Second, we need to stop treating students as customers and start treating them as members of the academic community.

Finally, drawing on the work of Carl Rogers, the chapter will conclude by identifying four rights that could form the basis of a freedom to learn. I will argue that these are quite modest and achievable proposals that are essential to implement if we are to reclaim the idea of what it means to be authentically student-centered.

Treating students as independent learners

In April 2009, the death was announced of Tyrrell Burgess, professor of the philosophy of social institutions and a radical educational thinker and innovator. Burgess believed in the individual nature of learning and the need to give students control over their own learning objectives where tutors work to actively support their needs (Burgess, 2000). He was the founding Director of the School for Independent Study that was set up at the North East London Polytechnic (now the University of East London) in 1974. In that year Burgess helped found a diploma in higher education on the basis of an independent learning approach. The course had 'no specified content, no prescribed reading lists, no timetables and no formal examinations' (Stephenson, 1993: 5). Students from a variety of social, economic and educational backgrounds, some of whom had previously been rejected by other institutions or expelled from school, planned their own course objectives and learning goals (Cunningham, 1999). By 1984, ten years on from the founding of the diploma, over one thousand students had graduated and the program enjoyed a completion rate similar to other more traditionally taught programs (Stephenson, 1993).

During the 1970s and 1980s there was considerable interest in the development of students as independent learners. Cowan (1978: 139) reports on a study funded by the Nuffield Foundation, for example, on the development of a 'course without a syllabus' as a means by which students might acquire greater autonomy. A range of terms and phrases gained popularity, such as 'learner-managed learning' (Graves, 1993). Being an independent learner, with proper support from expert tutors, well-resourced libraries and like-minded peers, was widely understood as the key to success at university and important in the development of student skills for employment. The focus was more about learning without lectures rather than the necessity of attendance. This philosophy was not based on an elitist view of higher education for the privileged few, such as the type enjoyed by Stephen Fry at Cambridge in the late 1970s (see Chapter 7). Nothing could be further from the truth. This was a vision for all students to have the opportunity to be trusted to learn independently. The varied socio-economic backgrounds of the students on the diplomas and honors degrees taking independent learning programs demonstrated this inclusive goal. Independent learning was about making higher education both more accessible and genuinely centered on the needs and interests of the learner.

Talk about independent learning in higher education has withered since the 1970s and 1980s. Critics were skeptical that a student's own educational objectives could be relied on to match the academic standards of more conventionally designed programs (Andresen *et al.*, 2000). Interest in independent learning has been largely displaced, or perhaps succeeded, by a literature on experience-based and, later, experiential learning. This latter approach has come to play a significant role within professional and practice-based degree programs and is strongly associated with citizenship education feeding into expectations of behavioral change that I have termed emotional performativity. As Burgess envisaged, the objectives of such programs are rarely determined by students as a way of giving them control of their own curriculum but controlled by institutions keen to promote cross-university themes related to service learning and global citizenship.

Yet, despite the fact that independent learning is no longer in fashion within the higher education literature, acquiring the qualities of an independent learner remains central to student freedom and student success at university and beyond. Independent learning is still the main basis of the higher education learning environment (Christie *et al.*, 2013). This is what enables students to gain autonomy and maturity as learners and helps them adjust to university life from more-directive and highly controlled school and college environments. Dispositions associated with being independent and making a successful transition into university life include acquiring good study habits, time management and taking 'more self-directed and independent approaches to academic work' (Krause and Coates, 2008: 500). Other research reinforces the continuing importance of being an independent learner at university:

> successful transitions depend on the students becoming independent learners . . . the students who adapt best to the new learning environment are those who understand what independent learning entails, and who are good time managers.
>
> (Christie *et al.*, 2013: 623)

Sometimes independent learning is mistakenly considered to be a 'soft' option without sufficient academic rigor. It is further common to misunderstand independent learning as a low-cost way of teaching by sending the student away to learn on their own. Neither of these criticisms holds much water if the responsibilities of providing adequate and flexible academic support to students is met. Helping students to learn independently is a highly demanding activity for the teacher, requiring considerable investment in understanding the student's personal and academic objectives and in-depth knowledge of their academic field. It perhaps explains why this approach has been overtaken by a culture of learning based on performativity in recent years since this is one more suited to mass participation systems with higher staff-student ratios. Academic managers can falsely see independent learning, commonly as part of distance or 'open' education, as a more economical way to manage large student numbers. Independent learning, though, does not mean sending students off without support to 'be independent' on their own. It means allowing learners to develop understanding *for themselves* as opposed to being told to simply go away and learn things *by themselves* (Mascolo, 2009: 7). This is a point which returns to some of the arguments I made in Chapter 5 about the way in which student-centered is misinterpreted. Moreover, academics know that independent learning is a time-consuming and demanding alternative to conventional methods and are not necessarily keen to embrace the concept on this basis (Jordan and Yeomans, 1991).

Independent learning is challenging not just for students but for teachers, since it entails giving up a degree of control over the curriculum. This process can be complex to manage and can even challenge the expertise of the academic as students control the direction and pace of their learning rather than the teacher. This is why academics have often shied away from the challenge of fostering an independent learning approach, preferring the comparative safety of the lecture, especially as a way of coping with large student numbers (Jordan and Yeomans, 1991). Increasing research intensity has become the prime focus of academic life since the mid-to-late 1980s, allied to the growth of audit exercises in several national higher education systems, performance in which is usually critical to promotion and career opportunities. This trend has had a further, negative impact on the radical and time-hungry demands of implementing independent learning.

Despite these problems, the principles of independent learning point clearly to what it means to offer a student-centered approach to learning at university. This does not necessitate an evangelical sweeping away of all conventional courses and methods. Instead it demands an understanding that there is a need to increase opportunities for students to be allowed to learn independently and to be given more freedom and choice in the curriculum than they are currently offered. It might include more emphasis on negotiated assignments and choice in undertaking either an individual or group-based assignment. These are not especially radical proposals but they are consistent with the principles of student-centeredness established by Carl Rogers.

Treating students *better* than customers

> The appearance of 'student consumerism' is a result of a realization that the student, because of his financial, time, and personal investment, is the prime consumer of postsecondary education.
>
> (Shulman, 1976: 2)

> Post-secondary institutions are faced with many questions regarding the value and effectiveness of their academic programs, heightened by the economic milieu of higher education and the rise of student consumerism.
>
> (Morstain, 1977: 1)

Considerable attention focuses on the debate about the 'student-as-consumer' (or customer), a metaphor that is representative of the shifting relationship between students and the university from one based on membership of an academic community to one founded on a contractual deal between a customer and a service provider. Much of what is written about this topic is presented as a recent phenomenon attributed to the prevalence of neo-liberal policies pursued by twenty-first-century governments who tend to evaluate higher education as an economic good bringing private benefits to individuals rather than as a public good or service. This has led today's writers and researchers on higher education to attribute a more 'customer'-oriented attitude to the student population as society increasingly sees universities in instrumental terms as just any other private service. In the UK, students have been encouraged to think of themselves as customers or, in the words of the Dearing report on higher education published in 1997, as 'investors', for at least the last 20 years: '[universities must] encourage the student to see him/herself as an investor in receipt of a service, and to seek, as an investor, value for money and a good return from the investment' (NCIHE, 1997: ch. 22, para. 19).

The tripling of student tuition fees in the UK in 2010 represents an important further watershed in shifting the public understanding of the purpose of higher education and the role of the student as a learner. Yet, claims about the student-as-consumer need to be understood with some historical perspective. As the above quotations from Shulman (1976) and Morstain (1977) illustrate, the student consumerism debate is at least 40 years old. In the nascent higher education of the late 1960s and 1970s there was plenty of interest in this topic (e.g. Dykstra, 1966; Peterson, 1970; El-Kalwass, 1976; Green, 1978). In an article from 1969, Johnstone uses the phrase 'student-as-consumer' in reference to students having the choice of electives (Johnstone, 1969). Back in 1967, Zinkin wondered whether the student-as-consumer would want to evaluate their lectures and tutorials on the basis of the same superficial criteria that might be applied to toilet soap. By the mid-1970s students were being widely recognized as 'objective consumers of the teaching process' (Grush and Costin, 1975: 55), and Joan Stark (1975) was bemoaning 'the new consumerism in higher education' while Pernal was asking 'Has student consumerism gone too far?' (Pernal, 1977: 2). Hence, the sense of moral panic about 'student consumerism' suggested by Pernal's question has been going on a very long time indeed. The collective hand-wringing has been around for as long as there has been a serious literature on higher education.

In the UK, there has been a tendency to attribute what is sometimes characterized as a rising tide of student consumerism to the neo-liberal policies pursued by the governments of Margaret Thatcher after 1979. Yet, in reality, the roots of student consumerism pre-date this period both in the UK and the US. In the UK, the Labour prime minister James Callaghan started to question the value and purpose of public education, and who should have a legitimate voice in such a debate, in his speech at Ruskin College, Oxford, in 1976. In the US, President John F. Kennedy's special message to Congress on consumer protection in the early 1960s is significant. The statement referred to the obligation of government to protect a consumer's rights: to safety, to be informed, to choose and to be heard (Kennedy, 1962). In his speech, Kennedy stated that measures would be taken to increase consumer protection in areas where citizens made costly purchases including the education of their children.

Students are 'consumers' of education but it does not necessarily follow that they either act like consumers or should be treated as such. The emphasis now placed on survey data in measuring the quality of the student experience focuses on their 'satisfaction' rather than their happiness (Dean and Gibbs, 2015). The notion of satisfaction is principally based on an investment model of higher education as representing value for money, while student happiness involves understanding the role of personal agency and self-motivation. Unfortunately, though, the persuasive power of the 'student-as-consumer' model dominates thinking about the student experience and how best to measure it. It has led to a tendency to blame students for 'consumer-like' behavior in choosing not to attend lectures or in demanding higher grades. Here we need to stop criticizing students for acting as consumers or 'customers'. If some students behave like customers it is because higher education institutions have made them into customers. Students who skip lectures or complain about their grades are simply acting rationally in a higher education system where they are over-assessed and given insufficient time and opportunity to study without the pressure of almost immediate assessment. It is also highly questionable whether there really was some kind of Golden Age when students wanted to work as hard as possible to obtain their degree. What seems more probable is that students are now more likely to act in a less deferential way. In most respects this is a healthy sign that we live in a society where authority is less likely to go unquestioned, something that has been remarked on since at least the 1960s, rather than one in which the power of professionals, including academics, goes meekly unchallenged. The academic community should be open to scrutiny and challenge by students, especially where it exposes poor or lazy teaching and unfair assessment practices.

Moreover, there has been a tendency to label any form of student complaint as evidence of student consumerism. It is inevitable that in a mass, as opposed to elite, system the number of such complaints will be higher. What is surprising is that complaints are still comparatively rare given the numbers of students studying at university. Much of the literature on the 'student-as-consumer' is opinion-based rather than empirical. That which is empirical tends to conflate the appearance of cases where students, or their parents, challenge the authority of academics and their institutions as evidence of a 'consumerist' mentality on a wider scale. Cases where students protest a grade or take a university to court are still proportionately very low, but they make good, sensationalist news stories. Accusations of so-called 'grade grubbing' often have more to do with academic defensiveness and a failure to mark fairly, particularly, as I have argued elsewhere in this book, where students are allocated the same grade on the basis of very different levels of contribution to group projects (see Chapter 5). These are legitimate grounds for complaint since basic principles of fairness or justice are too often seen as secondary to what constitutes 'effective' learning and teaching.

The truth is not that students are customers. This is a truism. What is more important to understand is that they are treated *worse* than customers. Students, or possibly their parents, pay for the privilege of a higher education, often via deferred debt schemes, and, rather than being treated with respect as autonomous adults, are subjected to a performative culture which seeks to measure their so-called engagement in terms of how much time and effort they are perceived to make in completing their studies. They are treated as children through the demands of bodily performativity, required to demonstrate their participative performativity in a one-size-fits-all 'active' learning approach, and, finally, patronized by the demands of emotional performativity. The performative culture of student learning makes insufficient allowance for diversity in the way in which students might prefer to learn. Higher education institutions cannot have it both ways. They cannot claim, on the one hand, that they treat students as customers and then, simultaneously, provide a service experience that takes no account of personal choice in what, when and how this learning takes place. This is no way to treat a customer who has paid for a service. If students are customers they should have the right to choose how they wish to engage with the service they are consuming.

There are other illustrations of the way in which students are treated worse than customers. One of these is in respect to their intellectual property rights (IPR). While universities commonly tend to claim ownership of the intellectual property of their professoriate, as employees of the institution, some, such as Plymouth University in the UK, attribute the IPR of students to themselves as well (Conran, 2014). Although the effect of such rules, particularly on most undergraduate students, may be negligible, those in advanced study or in creative areas, such as design, can be adversely affected. The situation is complicated by the fact that in some circumstances students might work creatively with professors. This attempt by institutions to claim ownership of student IPR is dubious from a legal standpoint (Patel, 1996). It is highly questionable from a moral standpoint too, as students, whether they are customers or not, are clearly not employees unless, perhaps, working as a temporary research or teaching assistant. Claiming ownership of the IPR of students is a classic example of universities treating their students worse than customers.

Student rights

The relationship between universities and the student population is one that has been increasingly 'hollowed out'. Treating students as customers, or stakeholders who need to be managed, has changed the basis of the relationship to one that is essentially contractual and transactional. This has ripped the heart out of a relationship that should be based on Rogerian principles such as empathy for and trust in the student. It is a relationship that can be recovered but only if we return to some the principles that Carl Rogers outlined in relation to what it means to be student-centered.

Right to non-indoctrination

Treating students better than customers means an engagement based on a culture of learning that is democratic and anti-authoritarian (Rogers, 1951: 387). Students need to enjoy what Rogers called 'inner freedom'; to be allowed to be themselves. This means ensuring that the 'threat to the self of the learner is reduced to a minimum' (1951: 391). It follows that students should have a *right to non-indoctrination* (Moshman, 2009) and not feel under pressure to align themselves with any one particular conceptual, theoretical or political perspective. This is a right threatened less by charismatic academics who might have commitments to particular normative positions and more by student engagement policies that promote socio-political agendas, such as global citizenship. The emotional performativity by which students are expected to demonstrate their compliance with such beliefs and values are more of a menace to their inner freedom than any left-wing (or right-wing) professor or through a curriculum that fails to adequately reflect the full range of theoretical and practice-based views and arguments within a discipline or professional practice subject.

Right to reticence

Rogers further emphasized how important it was to have a classroom that is free from emotional stress. Requiring oral contributions can be one the biggest causes of student stress. Rogers recognized this when he referred to the need for 'acceptance of his silence or talking' (1951: 395). A democratic approach is for the teacher to seek voluntary rather than compulsory contributions to class discussion. Emitted contributions, offered on a voluntary basis, differ significantly from elicited ones where the teacher 'calls out' a student by name demanding an oral comment from them. The student is, in effect, forced to speak even if they are reluctant to do so for whatever reason. Some might argue that relying purely on emitted responses runs the risk of a lack of participation or even silence in the classroom. The truth is that such a scenario occurs largely as a result of a lack of skill on the part of the teacher to encourage participation rather than reluctance for students to speak. It needs to be understood as a teaching deficit, not a student deficit. Moreover, if students do not wish to speak, why should they? As I argued in Chapters 4 and 5, students should have a *right to reticence*.

There is an increasing tendency to use student or audience response systems as a means of getting students to participate in class. These systems, often involving the use of clickers in class or available online, normally allow for anonymized responses, at the discretion of the teacher. Yet, even where student responses are anonymized, they are still deployed on the basis of an expectation that everyone in the class will participate. They are often seen as technologically supportive to active learning approaches and educationally unproblematic, but seek to extract responses from all students on an elicited rather than emitted basis. The fact that a student may not wish to make a contribution does not necessarily mean that they are not learning, or participating in class in other ways. Student response systems require participation and more often than not are used as a means for the teacher, and not the students, to set the agenda about what is worth discussing in the first place.

Right to choose how to learn

In Chapter 5, I argued that the way in which students engaged in class (or online) has been increasingly taken over by the assumptions of participative performativity. Here, there is a fundamental misunderstanding that students must be forced into an 'active' approach to learning as anything 'passive', including conventional forms of learning such as reading, denotes a lack of engagement. Such an approach is not student-centered since it robs the student of any choice in how they might prefer to learn. Rogers stated that 'if students are free, they should be free to learn passively as well as to initiate their own learning' (1951: 134). Students deserve the *right to choose how to learn* and not a one-size-fits-all approach. Here, while much educational research may have shown the benefits in students learning actively this does not mean that all students *have* to learn in this manner if they would prefer not to. Trying to maximize choice for students within the curriculum needs to be of prime concern in any student-centered approach to learning. While the full implications of independent learning may not be welcomed by all learners, there should be more emphasis on allowing and enabling students to make choices such as setting their own assignment or discussion topics.

At postgraduate research level, real choice is being increasingly hollowed out by institutional policies aimed at improving completion rates within tight timeframes. To some extent these are based on the needs of funding organizations, such as the UK Economic and Social Research Council (ESRC). Completion rates for PhDs funded by the ESRC have risen substantially as a result of tighter rules (ESRC, 2007). Yet, universities are now imposing stricter timeframes on all their research students, regardless of how they are funded, due to wider pressures connected with institutional reporting of completion statistics. At one level, more 'timely' completion by doctoral students might be regarded as indicating improved supervision and greater administrative efficiency. Yet, these shorter timeframes are restricting the freedom of students to pursue projects based on substantial data collection, longitudinal studies or work that is considered too complex or risky in a way that parallels the effects on academic faculty affected by periodic research audits such as the Research Excellence Framework in the UK. There is a scaling-back of ambition taking place. Here there is a negative impact on the scope and ambition of doctorates and an erosion of *real choice*, since research students are forced to compromise their intellectual ambitions on the basis of a bureaucratic requirement. While institutions have their hands tied by sponsors only prepared to fund a student for a limited period, where such restrictions are applied to those able to self-fund their studies this is another instance of students being treated in a way in which no business organization would dream of treating a customer if they wanted to retain their business. The scaling-back of ambition of what is intended to be a significantly challenging intellectual project is a further case of the way in which the purpose of a higher education is being driven by the demands of a performative culture rather than one that prioritizes student academic freedom.

Right to be trusted as an adult

Another fundamental principle of being student-centered is to trust the student. This depends, according to Rogers, on providing the right atmosphere in which a student is allowed to grow (1951: 427). There are a multiplicity of ways in which the university demonstrates its lack of trust in students, including compulsory attendance rules, attendance proxies, plagiarism checks on work ranging from undergraduate essays to doctoral theses and the use of technology to track engagement with online learning systems. Several of these examples are related to the effects of massified higher education where it is increasingly difficult for teaching faculty to know the individual student. Others, notably compulsory attendance rules, are further indicators of a failure to treat students as adults with sufficient maturity. They are symptomatic of a lack of trust in students as being capable of judging how best to use their own time and learn in ways which are not simple to observe and measure. The assumptions that inform this lack of trust in students are turning university teachers into surveillance officers rather than educators. This stands in stark contrast with the attributes that teachers need to exercise their role according to Rogerian principles that include congruence, unconditional positive regard and empathy (Blackie *et al.*, 2010). These principles demand that they relate to students in ways that are authentic and do not disguise their true selves. Teachers need to empathize with what it is like to be a student. This means placing themselves in the shoes of their own students. For instance, how many university professors or teachers were subject to the attendance rules now imposed on the current generation of university students when they were studying for their first degrees? There is a need for them to consider whether they would want to be treated in such a way. It is essential for university teachers not to forget what it was like to be a student, however distant that memory might be. In a mass system of higher education where it is increasingly difficult to get to know students as individuals, maintaining the capacity to understand what it is like to be a student is a vital way in which teaching can still be student or person-centered.

Student academic freedom needs to be understood in terms of both negative and positive rights. Non-indoctrination and reticence are both negative rights in the sense that they are about not having something taken away from the learner.

The right to non-indoctrination is about not having the freedom to form a personal perspective on a conceptual or ideological issue removed. The right to reticence is about protecting a student's privacy inasmuch as they may not wish to express an opinion or make a comment while in class. While these types of negative rights are very important in protecting student academic freedom, as I have sought to argue in this book, positive rights, or the development of capabilities, are equally so. This is because there is a need to think of the way in which rights help build the capacity of the individual to be able to exercise their academic freedom as a learner. The right to choose how to learn is about being given the opportunity to explore alternative ways of engaging with knowledge on the basis of personal preference. The right to be trusted as an adult means both a *freedom from* certain restrictions which tend to be associated with compulsory education (such as attendance rules) and a *freedom to* take responsibility for managing one's own time and working practices with appropriate levels of tutor support and guidance.

The four rights I have identified do not specifically include student political freedom. This is not because I regard this as any less important than other aspects of student academic freedom but because I am seeking in this book to focus on the concept of a freedom to learn. Within this context students should have a right to protest. As I argued in Chapter 2, student rights to political freedom should not be redefined and domesticated within institutional frameworks. A student-centered approach would allow students to set their own political agenda rather than having one imposed on them by the university's professoriate or management. This is not just about the exercise of freedom. Evidence further indicates that institutions are more likely to sit up and listen to students when they act independently. In South Korea, considerable rises in tuition fees led to student demonstrations and large-scale public rallies in 2011. Fees rose rapidly during the early 2000s and this issue became the rallying point of student activism, succeeding the previous focus on campaigning for democratization in Korean politics. As a result of these protests students now play a more meaningful role as student commissioners and make up around one-third of the members of a committee at institutions such as Seoul National University responsible for reviewing and setting fees (Shin *et al.*, 2014). While this may not mean that universities will cease to raise fees at all in the future, often linked to considerations of market positioning in a crowded market, they are perhaps more likely to exercise greater restraint.

The responsibilities of academic freedom

It is a moot point whether the opportunity to benefit from a higher education can be thought of as a right (see Chapter 2). Currently, it is not universally understood as such although arguably it is rapidly being accepted as such in many developed economies. If higher education is thought of as a right then it does not necessarily flow that obligations or duties can be attached to accessing its benefits (McCowan, 2013). A more common point of view is that rights do not come without responsibilities. Inevitably individuals will react differently to the oppor-tunities that a higher education affords them. Not all students will make best or most-constructive use of their time. Some will cheat in examinations and others will, less dramatically but perhaps more widely, simply fail to act with the matu-rity expected of an adult. Exercising rights and making choices in all aspects of life bring consequences and a better understanding of personal responsibility for one's own actions. Ultimately, in the most extreme scenario, this might include failing a course or program of study. Making mistakes, and hopefully learning from them, is simply part of life. Students are people, not a breed apart. What is needed to help them flourish, following Rogerian thinking, is an environment 'where the student can become a mature, fully functioning member of society through engaging in learning' (Blackie *et al.*, 2010: 638). This is an environment based on trust in the student.

Responsibility for creating and protecting an environment in which student academic freedom can thrive is a responsibility of academic faculty and the insti-tutions for which they work. It is the responsibility of those academics who themselves enjoy academic freedom to protect the freedom of others, notably their own students. Students, as well as their professors, have a responsibility to exercise their freedom in a manner which does not deny others their own. It is the mirror image of the student's right to non-indoctrination. This consid-eration applies both within the classroom and beyond, in listening, exercising tolerance and not denying others the opportunity to express their views. The privileges of such a freedom are always easier to define than its limits. Normally this is understood by reference to reasonable restrictions, usually including the use of insulting or threatening language. The main rule of thumb, though, is that the exercise of academic freedom should not result in a restriction of somebody else's freedom.

There are, of course, wider issues in relation to academic freedom that have not formed the main focus of analysis within this book. One of these issues is the extent to which students should use their political freedom in ways which might restrict the freedom of others or 'shut down' debate on sensitive issues. The 'no platform' policy of the UK National Union of Students that bans representatives from racist or fascist organizations speaking on campus is justified on the basis of protecting students from harm. It is important that the original intentions of such a policy are not lost in seeking to extend such restrictions to other controversial debates about issues such as feminism, abortion and Middle East politics. The privilege of academic freedom brings with it the responsibility to listen and criti-cally engage with other perspectives, not to act as a form of censorship.

Universities have an essential duty here to protect the academic free-dom of all members of their academic community, including academic staff and students, and to act as a focal point of open debate as part of advancing knowledge and public understanding. Here, there is a need for institutions to prioritize this duty over the expediency of public relations. Agreeing too readily to demands to ban controversial speakers in order to avoid adverse publicity or offending a vocal group of critics represents a failure of this duty. The duty of universities, and the professoriate, is to foster the critical rationality and tolerance of the views of others, virtues identified powerfully by Karl Popper in *The Open Society and Its Enemies* (1945). This responsibility is about a process being open to evaluating knowledge claims, no matter how tentative and potentially controversial, rather than closing down what can be studied and discussed. This critical but open mindset is the only essential behavioral virtue that higher education needs to develop in its students since it enables students to fully engage with knowledge on their own terms and not on someone else's. It ultimately makes students free to learn and free to make up their own minds.

Conclusion

Student performativity – bodily, participative and emotional – is a growing phenomenon in global higher education, undermining both a genuinely student-centered curriculum and the rights of students – to non-indoctrination, reticence, in choosing how to learn and in being treated like an adult. In common with a number of other educational concepts, such as learning outcomes, the idea of student-centered has been adapted and distorted in serving organizational objectives that are focused on efficiency and effectiveness to meet government-funded performance targets. A narrow and authoritarian interpretation of student-centered as active and collaborative learning has led to the phrase being associated with a 'tyranny of participation' (Gourlay, 2015: 402). The idea of student-centered needs to be reclaimed by higher education thinkers and practitioners in the way in which Rogers originally intended: as a liberating concept that promotes rather than impedes student freedom to learn.

Perhaps the best summation of how Carl Rogers understood a student's freedom is contained in a statement from a student who wrote the following having just completed one of his own student-centered courses:

> I felt completely free in this course. I could come in late and leave early. I could talk or be silent. I got to know a number of the students rather well. I was treated like a mature adult. I felt no pressure from you. I didn't have to please you; I didn't have to believe you. It was all up to me.
>
> (Rogers, 1951: 395)

Students are only too well aware that the phrase student-centered is used as a political slogan (Lea *et al.*, 2003) but in order to be faithful to the true meaning of this term there is a need to return to its democratic roots. It is simply about treating students as mature persons with rights, something that should be enjoyed by all university students. This is both a moral and a practical imperative that points up the responsibility of academics to protect and promote not just their own freedom but that of their students too.

References

Abasi, A.R. and Graves, B. (2008). Academic literacy and plagiarism: conversations with international graduate students and disciplinary professors, *Journal of English for Academic Purposes*, 7, 4, 221–233.

Allen, D. (1999). Desire to finish college: an empirical link between motivation and persistence, *Research in Higher Education*, 40, 461–485.

Allen, D.O. and Webber, D. J. (2010). Attendance and exam performance at university: a case study, *Research in Post-Compulsory Education*, 15, 1, 33–47.

American Association of University Professors (AAUP) (1915). *1915 Declaration of Principles on Academic Freedom and Academic Tenure.* http://www.aaup.org/NR/rdonlyres/A6520A9D-0A9A-47B3-B550-C006B5B224E7/0/1915Declaration.pdf (accessed 5 February 2012).

American Association of University Professors (AAUP) (2007). *Freedom in the Classroom.* https://graduate.asu.edu/sites/default/files/freedo-classrm-rpt.pdf (accessed 14 May 2012).

Andresen, L., Boud, D. and Cohen, R. (2000). Experience-based learning. In G. Foley (Ed.), *Understanding Adult Education and Training* (pp. 225–239). 2nd edition. Sydney: Allen & Unwin.

Andrews, J. and Jones, M. (2015). What's happening in 'their space'? Exploring the borders of formal and informal learning with undergraduate students of education in the age of mobile technologies, *Journal of Interactive Media in Education*, 1, 16, 1–10.

Asmar, C. (2005). Internationalising students: reassessing diasporic and local student difference, *Studies in Higher Education*, 30, 3, 291–230.

Asmar, C., Page, S. and Radloff, A. (2015). Exploring anomalies in indigenous student engagement: findings from a national Australian survey of undergraduates, *Higher Education Research and Development*, 34, 1, 15–29.

Astin, A.W. (1993). *What Matters in College? Four critical years revisited.* San Francisco: Jossey-Bass.

Astin, A.W. (2002). Higher education and the cultivation of citizenship. In D. Allman and M. Beaty (Eds.), *Cultivating Citizens* (pp. 91–102). Lanham, MD: Lexington Books.

Astin, A.W., Astin, H.S. and Lindholm, J.A. (2011). *Cultivating the Spirit: How college can enhance students' inner lives.* San Francisco: Jossey-Bass.

Attwood, R. (2009). Thanks very much for coming: you shall be rewarded, *Times Higher Education Supplement*, 10 September, 6.

Aviv, R. (2007). Don't be shy, *The New York Times*, 4 November, 4A26.

Ball, S. (2003). The teacher's soul and the terrors of performativity, *Journal of Education Policy*, 18, 2, 215–228.

Ball, S. (2012). The making of a neoliberal academic, *Research in Secondary Education*, 2, 1, 29–31.

Barnett, R. (1990). *The Idea of Higher Education*. Buckingham: Society for Research into Higher Education/Open University Press.

Barnett, R. (1999). The coming of the global village: a tale of two inquiries, *Oxford Review of Education*, 25, 3, 293–306.

Barrie, S.C. (2004). A research-based approach to generic graduate attributes policy, *Higher Education Research and Development*, 23, 3, 261–275.

Batson, J.G. (2008). *Her Oxford*. Nashville, TN: Vanderbilt University Press.

Bean, J.C. and Peterson, D. (1998). Grading classroom participation. In R.S. Anderson and B.W. Speck (Eds.), *Changing the Way We Grade Student Performance: Classroom assessment and the new learning paradigm* (pp. 33–40). San Francisco: Jossey-Bass.

Bellah, R., Madsen, R., Sullivan, W.M., Swidler, A. and Tipton, S.M. (1985). *Habits of the Heart: Individualism and commitment in American life*. New York: Harper.

Bennett, N., Lockyer, J., Mann, K., Batty, H., LaForet, K., Rethans, J.J. and Silver, I. (2004). Hidden curriculum in continuing medical education, *Journal of Continuing Education in the Health Professions*, 24, 3, 145–152.

Berlin, I. (1958). *Two Concepts of Liberty*. Oxford: Oxford University Press.

Berman, J. (2001). *Risky Writing: Self-disclosure and self-transformation in the classroom*. Amherst: University of Massachusetts Press.

Bissell, C. (1969). Academic freedom: the student version, *Queen's Quarterly*, 76, 2, 171–184.

Blackie, M.A.L., Case, J.M. and Jawitz, J. (2010). Student-centredness: the link between transforming students and transforming ourselves, *Teaching in Higher Education*, 15, 6, 637–646.

Blass, E. (2001). What's in a name? A comparative study of the traditional public university and the corporate university, *Human Resource Development International*, 4, 2, 153–172.

Bleakley, A. (2000). Writing with invisible ink: narrative, confessionalism and reflective practice, *Reflective Practice*, 1, 11–24.

Bloxham, S. and Boyd, P. (2007). *Developing Effective Assessment in Higher Education: A practical guide*. Maidenhead: Open University Press.

Boud, D. (2001). Using journal writing to enhance reflective practice, *New Directions for Adult and Continuing Education*, 90, 9–17.

Bourn, D., McKenzie, A. and Shiel, C. (2006). *The Global University: The role of the university*. London: Development Education Association.

Bowen, E., Price, T., Lloyd, S. and Thomas, S. (2005). Improving the quantity and quality of attendance data to enhance student retention, *Journal of Further and Higher Education*, 29, 4, 375–385.

Bradbury, M. (1975). *The History Man*. London: Secker and Warburg.

Brigham, M. (2011). Creating a global citizen and assessing outcomes, *Journal of Global Citizenship and Equity Education* 1, 1, 15–43.

Brown, R. (2013). *Everything for Sale? The marketization of UK higher education*. London: Routledge/Society for Research into Higher Education.

Brown, S. (1994). Assessment for learning, *Learning and Teaching in Higher Education*, 1, 1, 81–89.

Buchanan, R.W. and Rogers, M. (1990). Innovative assessment in large classes, *College Teaching*, 38, 2, 69–74.

Burgess, T. (2000). The logic of learning and its implications for higher education, *Higher Education Review*, 32, 2, 53–65.

Cain, S. (2013). *Quiet: The power of introverts in a world that can't stop talking*. New York: Broadway Books.

Canterbury Christ Church University (2010). *Attendance Policy*. http://www. canterbury. ac.uk/support/student-support-services/staff/guidance-procedures/ cccu-attendance-policy-nov10.pdf (accessed 30 January 2011).

Cardozier, V.R. (1968). Student power in medieval universities, *The Personnel and Guidance Journal*, 46, 10, 944–948.

Carey, P. (2013). Student engagement: stakeholder perspectives on course representation in university governance, *Studies in Higher Education*, 38, 9, 1290–1304.

Carless, D. (2015). *Excellence in University Assessment: Learning from award-winning practice*. London: Routledge.

Carter, A. (2001). *The Political Theory of Global Citizenship*. London and New York: Routledge.

Case, J. and Gunstone, R. (2003). Going deeper than deep and surface approaches: a study of students' perception of time, *Teaching in Higher Education*, 8, 1, 55–69.

Caverley, N., Cunningham, J.B. and MacGregor, J.N. (2007). Sickness presenteeism, sickness absenteeism, and health following restructuring in a public service organization, *Journal of Management Studies*, 44, 304–319.

Chan, C.K.Y. (2012). Exploring an experiential learning project through Kolb's Learning Theory using a qualitative research method, *European Journal of Engineering Education*, 37, 4, 405–415.

Chanock, K. (2010). The right to reticence, *Teaching in Higher Education*, 15, 5, 543–552.

Christie, H., Barron, P. and D'Annunzio-Green, N. (2013). Direct entrants in transition: becoming independent learners, *Studies in Higher Education*, 38, 4, 623–637.

Clarkeburn, H. and Kettula, K. (2012). Fairness and using reflective journals in assessment, *Teaching in Higher Education*, 17, 4, 439–452.

Clements, D.H. (1997). (Mis?)Constructing constructivism, *Teaching Children Mathematics*, 4, 198–200.

Clouder, L. and Hughes, C. (2012). Introduction. In L. Clouder, C. Broughan, S. Jewell and G. Steventon (Eds.), *Improving Student Engagement and Development through Assessment: Theory and practice in higher education* (pp. 1–3). New York and Abingdon: Routledge.

Coates, H. and McCormick, A.C. (Eds.) (2014). *Engaging University Students: International insights from system-wide studies*. Dordrecht: Springer.

Cohen, S. (1972). *Folk Devils and Moral Panics*. London: MacGibbon and Kee.

Coleman, J.S. (1977). The academic freedom and responsibilities of foreign scholars in African universities, *Issue: A Journal of Opinion*, 7, 2, 14–32.

Conrad, C.F. and Haworth, J.G. (1997). *Emblems of Quality in Higher Education: Developing and sustaining high-quality programs*. Boston, MA: Allyn and Bacon.

Conran, T. (2014). Time to rethink the intellectual property rights culture, *Times Higher Education*, 14 August. https://www.timeshighereducation.com/comment/opinion/time-to-rethink-the-intellectual-property-rights-culture/2015114.article (accessed 2 December 2015).

Cooper, C.L. (1998). The changing nature of work, *Community, Work and Family*, 1, 3, 313–317.

Cousin, G. (2010). Positioning postionality. In M. Savin-Baden and C.H. Major (Eds.), *New Approaches to Qualitative Research: Wisdom and uncertainty* (pp. 9–18). New York/Abingdon: Routledge.

Cousin, G., Sovic, S., Bourn, D., Grant, E. and Fanghanel, J. (2013). *Global Citizenship as a Graduate Attribute ESRC End of Award Report*. RES-451-26-0888. Swindon: ESRC.

Cowan, J. (1978). Freedom in the selection of course content: a case study of a course without a syllabus, *Studies in Higher Education*, 3, 2, 139–148.

Cunningham, I. (1999). *The Wisdom of Strategic Learning: The self managed learning solution*. 2nd edition. Aldershot: Gower.

Curtis, S. and Shani, N. (2002). The effect of taking paid employment during term-time on students' academic studies, *Journal of Further and Higher Education*, 26, 2, 129–138.

Danvers, E.C. (2015). Criticality's affective entanglements: rethinking emotion and critical thinking in higher education, *Gender and Education*, doi: 10.1080/09540253.2015.1115469

Dawson, S.P. (2006). Online forum discussion interactions as an indicator of student community, *Australasian Journal of Educational Technology*, 22, 4, 495–510.

De Figueiredo-Cowen, M. (2002). Latin American universities, academic freedom and autonomy: a long-term myth? *Comparative Education*, 38, 4, 471–484.

Dean, A. and Gibbs, P. (2015). Student satisfaction or happiness? A preliminary rethink of what is important in the student experience, *Quality Assurance in Education*, 23, 1, 5–19.

Deem, R. and Brehony, K.J. (2005). Management as ideology: the case of 'New Managerialism' in higher education, *Oxford Review of Education*, 31, 2, 217–235.

Delucchi, M. and Korgen, K. (2002). 'We're the customer – we pay the tuition': student consumerism among sociology undergraduate majors, *Teaching Sociology*, 30, 1, 100–107.

Department for Business, Innovation and Skills (DBIS) (2014). *Participation Rates in Higher Education: Academic years 2006/2007–2012/2013*. London: DBIS. https://www.gov.uk/government/uploads/system/uploads/attachment_data/file/347864/HEIPR_PUBLICATION_2012-13.pdf (accessed 3 May 2015).

Department for Business, Innovation and Skills (DBIS) (2015). *Fulfilling Our Potential: Teaching excellence, social mobility and student choice*. London: DBIS.

Dhimar, R. (2006). *Student Perceptions of Attendance and Engagement at University*. Learning and Teaching Institute: Sheffield Hallam University. http://www.academia.edu/171598/Student_Perceptions_of_Engagement_and_Attendance (accessed 26 July 2015).

Dill, J.S. (2013). *The Longings and Limits of Global Citizenship Education: The moral pedagogy of schooling in a cosmopolitan age*. London and New York: Routledge.

Ditcher, A.K. (2001). Effective teaching and learning in higher education, with particular reference to the undergraduate education of professional engineers, *International Journal of Engineering Education*, 17, 1, 24–29.

Dixon, D. (1986). Teaching composition to large classes, *Forum*, 24, 3, 2–5.

Dolnicar, S. (2005). Should we still lecture or just post examination questions on the web? The nature of the shift towards pragmatism in undergraduate lecture attendance, *Quality in Higher Education*, 11, 2, 103–115.

Dolnicar, S., Kaiser, S., Matus, K. and Vialle, W. (2009). Can Australian universities take measures to increase the lecture attendance of marketing students? *Journal of Marketing Education*, 31, 203–211.

Dykstra, J.W. (1966). Consumer protection in the higher education marketplace, *Phi Delta Kappan*, 47, 446–448.

Economic and Social Research Council (ESRC) (2007). *Annual Reports and Accounts, 2006–2007*. London: The Stationery Office.

Edmond, N. and Berry, J. (2014). Discourses of 'equivalence' in HE and notions of student engagement: resisting the neoliberal university, *Student Engagement and Experience Journal*, 3, 2. http://dx.doi.org/10.7190/seej.v3i2.90 (accessed 14 February 2015).

Einaudi, L. (1963). University autonomy and academic freedom in Latin America, *Law and Contemporary Problems*, 28, 636–646.

El-Kalwass, E. (1976). Consumerism as an emerging issue for post-secondary education, *Educational Record*, 56, Spring, 126–131.

Entwistle, N. J. and Ramsden, P. (1983). *Understanding Student Learning*. Beckenham: Croom Helm.

Eraut, M. (2000). Non-formal learning and tacit knowledge in professional work, *British Journal of Educational Psychology*, 70, 113–136.

Eriksen, T.H. (2001). *Tyranny of the Moment: Fast and slow time in the information age*. London: Pluto Press.

Evans, C., Muijs, D. and Tomlinson, M. (2016). *Engaged Student Learning: High-impact strategies to enhance student achievement*. York: Higher Education Academy. https://www.heacademy.ac.uk/sites/default/files/engaged_student_learning_high-impact_pedagogies.pdf (accessed 4 February 2016).

Evans, J. (2013). Student protest has been quietly sweeping the nation. Now, it's getting louder, *New Statesman*, 14 December. http://www.newstatesman.com/politics/2013/12/student-protest-has-been-quietly-sweeping-nation-now-its-getting-louder (accessed 15 November 2014).

Fejes, A. and Dahlstedt, M. (2013). *The Confessing Society: Foucault, confession and practices of lifelong learning*. Oxford and New York: Routledge.

Fernex, A., Lima, L. and de Vries, E. (2015). Exploring time allocation for academic activities by university students in France, *Higher Education*, 69, 399–420.

Flint, R.A. and Johnson, B. (2011). *Towards Fairer University Assessment: Recognizing the concerns of students*. Oxford and New York: Routledge.

Foucault, M. (1977). *Discipline and Punishment*. London: Tavistock.

Foucault, M. (1978). *The History of Sexuality, Vol. 1: The will to knowledge*. Trans. R. Hurley. London: Penguin Books.

Frambach, J.M., Driessen, E.W., Beh, P. and van der Vieuten, C.P.M. (2013). Quiet or questioning? Students' discussion behaviors in student-centered education across cultures, *Studies in Higher Education*, 39, 6, 1001–1021.

Fredricks, J.A., Blumenfeld, P.C. and Paris, A.H. (2004). School engagement: potential of the concept, state of the evidence, *Review of Educational Research*, 74, 1, 59–109.

Friedman, P., Rodriguez, F. and McComb, J. (2001). Why students do and do not attend classes: myths and realities, *College Teaching*, 49, 124–133.

Fritschner, L.M. (2000). Inside the undergraduate college classroom: faculty and students differ on the meaning of student participation, *The Journal of Higher Education*, 71, 3, 342–362.

Fry, S. (2010). *The Fry Chronicles: An autobiography*. London: Michael Joseph.

Furedi, F. (2004). *Therapy Culture: Cultivating vulnerability in an uncertain age*. London and New York: Routledge.

Fusaro, M. and Couture, A. (2012). *Étude sur les modalités d'apprentissage et les technologies de l'information et de la communication dans l'enseignement*, Quebec: Conference Des Recteurs Et Des Principaux Des Universités Du Québec.

Gallagher, P.J. and Demos, G.D. (Eds.) (1983). *Handbook of Counseling in Higher Education*. New York: Praeger.

Garnett R. F. (2009). Liberal learning as freedom: a capabilities approach to undergraduate education, *Studies in Philosophy and Education*, 28, 5, 437–447.

Gendron, P. and Pieper, P. (2005). *Does Attendance Matter? Evidence from an Ontario ITAL discussion paper*. Toronto: The Business School, Humber Institute of Technology and Advanced Learning. http://economics.ca/2005/papers/0483.pdf (accessed 27 November 2012).

Gewirth, A. (1996). *The Community of Rights*. Chicago: The University of Chicago Press.

Gilbert, T. (2001). Reflective practice and clinical supervision: meticulous rituals of the confessional, *Journal of Advanced Nursing*, 36, 2, 199–205.

Glendinning, I. (2014). Responses to student plagiarism in higher education across Europe, *International Journal for Educational Integrity*, 10, 1, 4–20.

Goffman, E. (1959). *The Presentation of Self in Everyday Life*. New York: Doubleday.

Goleman, D. (1995). *Emotional Intelligence*. New York: Bantam Books.

Gourlay, L. (2015). Student engagement and the tyranny of participation, *Teaching in Higher Education*, 20, 4, 402–411.

Graham, C.R., Tripp, T.R., Seawright, L. and Joeckel, G.L. (2007). Empowering or compelling reluctant participators using audience response systems, *Active Learning in Higher Education*, 8, 3, 233–258.

Graves, N. (Ed.) (1993). *Learner Managed Learning: Practice, theory and policy*, London and New York: Routledge.

Green, S. (1978). Students as consumers: the need for better information, *Journal of Indiana University Student Personnel Association*, 4–8.

Gregory, D., Johnston, R., Pratt, G., Watts, M. and Whatmore, S. (2011). *The Dictionary of Human Geography*. Chichester: Wiley.

Grin, B. (2004). Putting past behind him, Ted Turner '60 builds strong relationship with university, *The Brown Daily Herald*, 20 September.

Grush, J.E. and Costin, F. (1975). The student as consumer of the teaching process, *American Educational Research Journal*, 12, 1, 55–66.

Gulati, S. (2008). Compulsory participation in online discussions: is this constructivism or normalisation of learning? *Innovations in Education and Teaching International*, 45, 2, 183–192.

Gullifer, J. and Tyson, G.A. (2010). Exploring university students' perceptions of plagiarism: a focus group study, *Studies in Higher Education*, 35, 4, 463–481.

Hall, M. (2008). Getting to know the feral learner. In J. Visser and M. Visser-Valfrey (Eds.), *Learners in a Changing Landscape: Reflections from a discipline on new roles and expectations* (pp. 109–134). Dordrecht: Springer.

Hall, M. (2015). Rhodes' statue falls but toxic legacy lingers, *Times Higher Education*, 16 April.

Halsey, A. and Trow, M. (1971). *The British Academics*. London: Faber and Faber.

Hanbury, A., Prosser, M. and Rickinson, M. (2008). The differential impact of UK accredited teaching development programmes on academics' approaches to teaching, *Studies in Higher Education*, 33, 4, 469–483.

Hancock, D. (2004). Cooperative learning and peer orientation effects on motivation and achievement, *The Journal of Educational Research*, 97, 3, 159–166.

Hanson, K. (1996). Between apathy and advocacy: teaching and modeling ethical reflection, *New Directions for Teaching and Learning*, 66, 33–36.

Harland, T., McClean, A., Wass, R., Miller, E. and Kwong, N.S. (2015). An assessment arms race and its fallout: high-stakes grading and the case for slow scholarship, *Assessment & Evaluation in Higher Education*, 40, 4, 528–541.

Harumi, S. (2010). Classroom silence: voices from Japanese EFL learners, *English Language Teaching Journal*, 65, 1, 1–10.

Haworth, J. and Conrad, C. (1997). *Emblems of Quality: Developing and sustaining high quality programs*. Boston, MA: Allyn and Bacon.

HEAR (Higher Education Achievement Report) (2015). *About the HEAR*. http://www.hear.ac.uk/about (accessed 10 December 2015).

HEPI (Higher Education Policy Institute)/Which? (2013). *The Student Academic Experience Survey*. London: Which?/HEPI.

Heriot Watt University (2007). *Policy on Student Attendance*. http://www.hw.ac.uk/registry/resources/studentattendancepolicy.pdf (accessed 10 February 2011).

Hobbs, V. (2007). Faking it or hating it: can reflective practice be forced? *Reflective Practice*, 8, 3, 405–417.

Hodgson, K. (2013). We must never allow gender segregation at our universities for any reason, *The Independent*, 17 December. http://www.independent.co.uk/student/istudents/we-must-never-allow-gender-segregation-at-our-universities-for-any-reason-9009886.html (accessed 20 December 2013).

Hoefer, C. (2013). Students feel the stress of higher demands, *The Volante*, 9 October. http://www.volanteonline.com/news/students-feel-the-stress-of-higher-demands/article_9a5313f6-30b6-11e3-a942-001a4bcf6878.html (accessed 22 July 2014).

Holmes, L. (2004). Challenging the learning turn in education and training, *Journal of European Industrial Training*, 28, 8/9, 625–638.

Horn, M. (1999). Students and academic freedom in Canada, *Historical Studies in Education*, 11, 1, 1–32.

Horowitz, D. (2002). *Academic Bill of Rights*. Washington, DC: Students for Academic Freedom. http://www.sturights.org (accessed 12 February 2013).

Hounsell, D. (2011). *Graduates for the 21st Century: Integrating the enhancement themes*. Glasgow: Quality Assurance Agency for Higher Education, Glasgow. http://www.enhancementthemes.ac.uk/ (accessed 7 October 2013).

Howie, P. and Bagnall, R. (2013). A critique of the deep and surface approaches to learning model, *Teaching in Higher Education*, 18, 4, 389–400.

Hyde, C.A. and Ruth, B.J. (2002). Multicultural content and class participation: do students self-censor? *Journal of Social Work Education*, 38, 2, 241–256.

Ison, D.C. (2012). Plagiarism among dissertations: prevalence at online institutions, *Journal of Academic Ethics*, 10, 3, 227–236.

Jackson, B. (1991). The lingering legacy of in loco parentis: an historical survey and proposal for reform, *Vanderbilt Law Review*, 44, 1135–1164.

Jackson, P.W. (1968) *Life in Classrooms*. New York: Teachers College Press.

Jamieson, P. (2009). The serious matter of informal learning, *Planning for Higher Education*, 37, 2, 18–24.

Jin, J. (2012). Sounds of silence: examining silence in problem-based learning (PBL) in Asia. In S. Bridges, C. McGrath and T. Whitehill (Eds.), *Problem-Based Learning in Clinical Education: The next generation* (pp. 171–185). Dordrecht: Springer.

Johnstone, D.B. (1969). The student and his power, *The Journal of Higher Education*, 40, 3, 205–218.

Jones, J., Gaffney-Rhys, R. and Jones, E. (2012). Handle with care! An exploration of the potential risks associated with the publication and summative usage of student evaluation of teaching (SET) results, *Journal of Further and Higher Education*, 38, 1, 37–56.

Jordan, S. and Yeomans, D. (1991). Whither independent learning? The politics of curricular and pedagogical change in a polytechnic department, *Studies in Higher Education*, 16, 3, 291–308.

Kahu, E.R. (2013). Framing student engagement in higher education, *Studies in Higher Education*, 38, 5, 758–773.

Kandlbinder, P. and Peseta, T. (2009). Key concepts in postgraduate certificates in higher education teaching and learning in Australasia and the United Kingdom, *International Journal for Academic Development*, 14, 1, 19–31.

Karran, T. (2009). Academic freedom: in justification of a universal ideal, *Studies in Higher Education*, 34, 3, 263–283.

Katz, E. and Rosenberg, J. (2005). An economic theory of volunteering. *European Journal of Political Economy*, 21, 2, 429–443.

Keddie, A. (2016). Children of the market: performativity, neoliberal responsibilisation and the construction of student identities, *Oxford Review of Education*, doi: 10.1080/03054985.2016.1142865

Kelly, G. (2012). Lecture attendance rates at university and related factors. *Journal of Further and Higher Education*, 36, 1, 17–40.

Kember, D. (2004). Interpreting student workload and the factors which shape students' perceptions of their workload, *Studies in Higher Education*, 29, 2, 165–184.

Kennedy, J.F. (1962). Special message to the Congress on protecting the consumer interest, March 15, 1962. http://www.presidency.ucsb.edu/ws/?pid=9108 (accessed 18 March 2014).

Kettle, M. (2011). Academic practice as explanatory framework: reconceptualising international student academic engagement and university teaching, *Discourse: Studies in the Cultural Politics of Education*, 32, 1, 1–14.

King, P.E. and Behnke, R.R. (2005). Problems associated with evaluating student performance in groups, *College Teaching*, 53, 2, 57–61.

Kirschner, P.A., Sweller, J. and Clark, R.E. (2006). Why minimal guidance during instruction does not work: an analysis of the failure of constructivist, discovery, problem-based, experiential, and inquiry-based teaching, *Educational Psychologist*, 41, 2, 75–86.

Klemenčič, M. (2012). The changing conceptions of student participation in HE governance in the EHEA. In A. Curaj, P. Scott, L. Vlasceanu and L. Wilson (Eds.),

European Higher Education at the Crossroads: Between the Bologna process and national reforms (pp. 631–652). Dordrecht: Springer.

Kneale P. (1997). The rise of the 'strategic student': how can we adapt to cope? In S. Armstrong, G. Thompson G. and S. Brown (Eds.), *Facing Up to Radical Changes in Universities and Colleges* (pp. 119–130). London: Kogan Page/SEDA.

Ko, S.-S. (2014). Peer assessment in group projects accounting for assessor reliability by an iterative method, *Teaching in Higher Education*, 19, 3, 301–314.

Krause, K.-L. and Coates, H. (2008). Students' engagement in first-year university, *Assessment & Evaluation in Higher Education*, 33, 5, 493–505.

Kuh, G.D., Cruce, T.M., Shoup, R., Kinzie, J. and Gonyea, R.M. (2008). Unmasking the effects of student engagement on first-year college grades and persistence, *Journal of Higher Education*, 79, 5, 540–563.

Lasch, C. (1979). *The Culture of Narcissism: American life in the age of diminishing expectations.* London and New York: Norton Press.

Latane, B., Williams, K. and Harkins, B. (1979). Many hands make light the work: the causes and consequences of social loafing, *Journal of Personality and Social Psychology*, 37, 822–832.

Law, D.W. (2007). Exhaustion in university students and the effect of coursework involvement, *Journal of American College Health*, 55, 4, 239–245.

Lea, S.J., Stephenson, D. and Troy, J. (2003). Higher education students' attitudes to student-centred learning: beyond 'educational bulimia'?, *Studies in Higher Education*, 28, 3, 321–334.

Leufer, T. and Cleary-Holdforth, J. (2010). Reflections on the experience of mandating lecture attendance in one school of nursing in the Republic of Ireland, *All Ireland Journal of Teaching and Learning in Higher Education*, 2, 1, 18.1–18.14.

Little, B., Locke, W., Scesa, A. and Williams, R. (2009). *Report to the HEFCE on Student Engagement.* Bristol: Higher Education Funding Council for England.

Little, G. (1970). *Faces on the Campus: A psycho-social study.* Carlton: Melbourne University Press.

Livingstone, D. and Lynch, K. (2000). Group project work and student-centred active learning: two different experiences, *Studies in Higher Education*, 25, 3, 325–245.

Long, D.D. and Bedard, J.C. (1985). Evaluation of a discussion technique used for both classroom instruction and grade assignment, *American Journal of Physics*, 53, 5, 401–404.

Lucas, L. (2006). *The Research Game in Academic Life.* Buckingham: Society for Research into Higher Education and Open University Press.

Luescher-Mamashela, L.M. (2010). From university democratisation to managerialism: the changing legitimation of university governance and the place of students, *Tertiary Education and Management*, 16, 4, 259–263.

Lusk, A.B. and Weinberg, A.S. (1994). Discussing controversial topics in the classroom: creating a context for learning, *Teaching Sociology*, 22, 301–308.

LV (2012). Total cost of university set to hit £53,330 per student. http://www.lv.com/adviser/working-with-lv/news_detail/?articleid=2984421 (accessed 9 August 2014).

Lyons, K., Hanley, J., Wearing, S. and Neil, J. (2012). Gap year volunteer tourism: myths of global citizenship? *Annals of Tourism Research*, 39, 1, 361–378.

Lyotard, J.-F. (1984). *The Postmodern Condition: A report on knowledge.* Minneapolis, MN: The University of Minnesota Press.

Macfarlane, B. (2000). Inside the corporate classroom, *Teaching in Higher Education*, 5, 1, 51–60.

Macfarlane, B. (2001). Developing reflective students: evaluating the benefits of learning logs within a business ethics programme, *Teaching Business Ethics*, 5, 4, 375–387.

Macfarlane, B. (2013). The surveillance of learning: a critical analysis of university attendance policies, *Higher Education Quarterly*, 67, 4, 358–373.

Macfarlane, B. (2015a). Student performativity in higher education: converting learning as a private space into a public performance, *Higher Education Research and Development*, 34, 2, 338–350.

Macfarlane, B. (2015b). Dualisms in higher education: a critique of their influence and effect, *Higher Education Quarterly*, 69, 1, 101–118.

Macfarlane, B. (2016). 'If not now, then when? If not us, who?' Understanding the student protest movement in Hong Kong. In R. Brooks (Ed.), *Student Politics and Protest: International perspectives* (pp. 143–156). London and New York: Routledge.

Macfarlane, B. and Gourlay, L. (2009). The reflection game: enacting the penitent self, *Teaching in Higher Education*, 14, 4, 455–459.

Machemer, P.L. and Crawford, P. (2007). Student perceptions of active learning in a large cross-disciplinary classroom, *Active Learning in Higher* Education, 8, 1, 9–30.

Malcolm, J. and Zukas, M. (2001). Bridging pedagogic gaps: conceptual discontinuities in higher education, *Teaching in Higher Education*, 6, 1, 33–42.

Marton, F. and Säljö, R. (1976). On qualitative differences in learning: outcome and process, *British Journal of Educational Psychology*, 46, 4–11.

Mascolo, M F. (2009). Beyond teacher- and learner-centered pedagogy: learning as guided participation, *Pedagogy and the Human Sciences*, 1, 4–27.

Matthews, D. (2015). Oxford college agrees to remove Cecil Rhodes plaque, *Times Higher Education*, 18 December.

McCormick, A.C. and Kinzie, J. (2014). Refocusing the quality discourse: the United States National Survey of Student Engagement. In H. Coates and A.C. McCormick (Eds.), *Engaging University Students: International insights from system-wide studies* (pp. 13–30). Dordrecht: Springer.

McCormick, R.E. and Meiners, R.E. (1988). University governance: a property rights perspective, *Journal of Law and Economics*, 31, 2, 423–442.

McCowan, T. (2010). Reframing the universal right to education, *Comparative Education*, 46, 4, 509–525.

McCowan, T. (2013). *Education as a Human Right: Principles for a universal entitlement to learning*. London and New York: Bloomsbury.

McDaniel, P.A. (2001). Shrinking violets and casper milquetoasts: shyness and heterosexuality from the roles of the fifties to the rules of the nineties, *Journal of Social History*, 34, 3, 547–568.

McGill, I. and Warner Weil, S. (1989). Continuing the dialogue: new possibilities for experiential learning. In S. Warner Weil and I. McGill (Eds.), *Making Sense of Experiential Learning* (pp. 245–274). Milton Keynes: Society for Research into Higher Education/Open University Press.

Metzger, W.P. (1987). Profession and constitution: two definitions of academic freedom in America, *Texas Law Review*, 66, 1265–1322.

Meyer, J.W. and Rowan, B. (1977). Institutionalized organizations: formal structure as myth and ceremony, *American Journal of Sociology*, 83, 340–363.

Middlesex University (2011). *Attendance (Pre-Registration Nursing and Midwifery) Policy.* unihub.mdx.ac.uk/Assets/attendance.docx (accessed 7 November 2013).

Millington, K. (2005). Gap year travel: international. *Travel and Tourism Analyst*, 12, 1–50.

Million + (2012). *Teaching that Matters.* http://www.millionplus.ac.uk/documents/reports/TTM_FINAL.pdf (accessed 14 December 2014).

Missouri State University (2012). *Attendance Policy.* http://www.missouristate.edu/registrar/attendan.html. (accessed 8 August 2012).

Monypenny, P. (1963). Toward a standard for student academic freedom, *Law and Contemporary Problems*, 28, 3, 625–635.

Moon, J. (2004). *A Handbook of Reflective and Experiential Learning: Theory and practice.* New York and London: Routledge.

Morrison, K. (1996). Developing a reflective practice in higher degree students through a learning journal, *Studies in Higher Education*, 21, 3, 317–332.

Morstain, B. (1977). An analysis of students' satisfaction with their academic program, *Journal of Higher Education*, 48, 1, 1–16.

Mortiboys, A. (2002). *The Emotionally Intelligent Lecturer.* Birmingham, UK: Staff and Educational Development Association.

Moshman, D. (2009) *Liberty and Learning: Academic freedom for teachers and students.* Portsmouth, NH: Heinemann.

Murray, J. (2012). Performativity cultures and their effects on teacher educators' work, *Research in Teacher Education*, 2, 2, 19–23.

National Committee of Inquiry into Higher Education (NCIHE) (1997). *Higher Education in the Learning Society.* London: HMSO.

National Union of Students (NUS) (2008). *NUS Student Experience Report.* NUS: London. http://www.nus.org.uk/PageFiles/4017/NUS_StudentExperience Report.pdf (accessed 13 March 2014).

Nelson, C. (2010). *No University Is an Island: Saving academic freedom.* New York: New York University Press.

Nelson, K.J., Quinn, C., Marrington, A. and Clarke, J.A. (2012). Good practice for enhancing the engagement and success of commencing students, *Higher Education*, 63, 1, 83–96.

Nesi, H. (2008).The form, meaning and purpose of university level assessed reflective writing. In M. Edwardes (Ed.), *Proceedings of the BAAL Annual Conference 2007.* London: Scitsiugnil Press.

Newswander, L.K. and Borrego, M. (2009). Engagement in two interdisciplinary graduate programs, *Higher Education*, 58, 4, 551–562.

Ni Raghallaigh, M. and Cunniffe, R. (2013). Creating a safe climate for active learning and student engagement: an example from an introductory social work module, *Teaching in Higher Education*, 18, 1, 93–105.

Nicol, D. (2010). *The Foundation for Graduate Attributes: Developing self-regulation through self and peer assessment.* Scotland, Glasgow: The Quality Assurance Agency for Higher Education. http://www.enhancementthemes.ac.uk (accessed 17 June 2012).

Nixon, J., Beattie, M., Challis, M. and Walker, M. (1998). What does it mean to be an academic? A colloquium, *Teaching in Higher Education*, 3, 3, 277–298.

Nonnecke, B. and Preece, J. (2000). *Lurker Demographics: Counting the silent.* *Proceedings of CHI 2000.* The Hague: ACM.

Norton, A.O. (1909). *Readings in the History of Education: Mediaeval universities.* Cambridge, MA: Harvard University Press.

Nussbaum, M.C. (2003). Capabilities as fundamental entitlements: Sen and social justice, *Feminist Economics*, 2–3, 3–59.

O'Donovan, B., Price, M. and Rust, C. (2004). Know what I mean? Enhancing student understanding of assessment standards and criteria, *Teaching in Higher Education*, 9, 3, 325–335.

O'Neil, O. (2002). *A Question of Trust: The BBC Reith Lectures 2002.* Cambridge: Cambridge University Press.

Oxfam (2013). *Global Citizenship.* http://www.oxfam.org.uk/education/global-citizenship (accessed 15 March 2014).

Parker, J. and Crona, B. (2012). On being all things to all people: boundary organizations and the contemporary research university, *Social Studies of Science*, 42, 2, 262–289.

Parry, M. and Malcolm, D. (2004). England's barmy army: commercialization, masculinity and nationalism, *International Review for the Sociology of Sport*, 39, 1, 75–94.

Patel, S.H. (1996). Graduate students' ownership and attribution rights in intellectual property. *Indiana Law Journal*, 71, 2. http://law.indiana.edu/ilj/volumes/v71/no2/patel.html (accessed 20 March 2010).

Penn State University. (2013). *Principles of Student Participation in Academic Affairs.* http://senate.psu.edu/policies/index.html (accessed 4 January 2014).

Pernal, M. (1977). Has student consumerism gone too far? *College Board Review*, 104, Summer, 2–5.

Peterson, R. (1970). The college catalog as a contract, *Educational Record*, 51, Summer, 260–266.

Pfaff, E. and Huddlestone, P. (2003). Does it matter if I hate teamwork? What impacts student attitudes towards teamwork, *Journal of Marketing Education*, 25, 1, 37–45.

Popper, K.R. (1945). *The Open Society and Its Enemies: Volume 1: The Spell of Plato.* London: Routledge and Kegan Paul.

Power, M. (1994). *The Audit Explosion.* London: Demos.

Power, M. (1997). *The Audit Society: Rituals of verification.* Oxford: Oxford University Press.

Rainer, T. (1978). *The New Diary.* New York: G. P. Putnam.

Reda, M.M. (2009). *Between Speaking and Silence: A study of quiet students.* New York: SUNY Press.

Reda, M. (2010). What's the problem with quiet students? Anyone? Anyone? *The Chronicle of Higher Education*, 5 September.

Richardson, J.T.E. (2014). Coursework versus examinations in end-of-module assessment: a literature review, *Assessment & Evaluation in Higher Education*, doi: 10.1080/02602938.2014.919628

Rochford, F. (2008). The contested product of a university education, *Journal of Higher Education Policy and Management*, 30, 1, 41–52.

Rochford, F. (2014). Bringing them into the tent: student association and the neutered academy, *Studies in Higher Education*, 39, 3, 485–499.

Roderick, C. (2010). Commodifying self: a grounded theory study, *The Grounded Theory Review*, 9, 1, 41–64.

Roddick, M. (2007). *Global Citizenship Perspectives: A case study of the WUSC international seminar*. https://devcase.org/documents/global-citizenship-perspectives. pdf (accessed 21 March 2012).

Rogers, C. (1951). *Client-Centered Therapy: Its current practice, implications and theory*. London: Constable.

Rogers, C. (1969). *Freedom to Learn: A view of what education might become*. Columbus, OH: Merrill Publishing.

Rogers, J.R. (2001). *A Panel-Data Study of the Effect of Student Attendance on University Performance*. http://ro.uow.edu.au/commpapers/171 (accessed 15 February 2011).

Rolfe, R. and Gardner, L. (2006) 'Do not ask who I am . . . ': confession, emancipation and (self)-management through reflection, *Journal of Nursing Management*, 14, 593–600.

Rose, N. (1990). *Governing the Soul: The shaping of the private self*. London: Routledge.

Ross, J. (2011). Traces of self: online reflective practices and performances in higher education, *Teaching in Higher Education*, 16, 1, 113–126.

Ross, J. (2014). Performing the reflective self: audience awareness in high-stakes reflection, *Studies in Higher Education*, 39, 2, 219–232.

Roulin, N. and Bangerter, A. (2013). Students' use of extra-curricular activities for positional advantage in competitive job markets, *Journal of Education and Work*, 26, 1, 21–47.

Russell, C. (1993). *Academic Freedom*. London: Routledge.

Sadler, D.R. (1987). Specifying and promulgating achievement standards, *Oxford Review of Education*, 13, 191–209.

Sadler, D.R. (2010). Fidelity as a precondition for integrity in grading academic achievement, *Assessment and Evaluation in Higher Education*, 35, 6, 727–743.

Salzman, S., Denner, P. and Harris, L. (2002). Teaching education outcomes measures: special study survey. Paper presented at the Annual Meeting of the American Association of Colleges of Teacher Education, New York. http://files.eric.ed.gov/fulltext/ED465791.pdf (accessed 15 March, 2015).

Sander, P., Stevenson, K., King, M. and Coates, D. (2000). University students' expectations of teaching, *Studies in Higher Education*, 25, 3, 309–323.

Sartre, J.-P. (1956). *Being and Nothingness: An essay on phenomenological ontology*. Trans. Hazel E. Barnes. New York: Philosophical Library.

Schön, D.A. (1983). *The Reflective Practitioner*. New York: Basic Books.

Schön, D.A. (1991). *The Reflective Turn: Case studies in and on educational practice*. New York: Teachers College.

Schrecker, E. (2010). *The Lost Soul of Higher Education: Corporatization, the assault on academic freedom and the American university*. New York: The New Press.

Scott, P. (1995). *The Meanings of Mass Higher Education*. Maidenhead: McGraw-Hill.

Scott, S. (2006). The medicalisation of shyness: from social misfits to social fitness, *Sociology of Health and Illness*, 28, 2, 133–153.

Seale, J. (2010). Doing student voice work in higher education: the potential contribution of a participatory framework, *British Educational Research Journal*, 36, 995–1015.

Sen, A. (1999). *Development as Freedom*. Oxford: Oxford University Press.

Sheridan, J., Bryan-Kinns, N., Reeves, S., Marshall, J. and Lane, G. (2011). Graffito: crowd-based performative interaction at festivals. In *Proceedings of CHI Conference on Human Factors in Computing Systems, 2011*, ACM, 1129–1134.

Shin, J.C., Kim, H.H. and Choi, H.S. (2014). The evolution of student activism and its influence on tuition fees in South Korean universities, *Studies in Higher Education*, 39, 3, 441–454.

Shulman, C.H. (1976). Student consumerism: caveat emptor reexamined, *Research Currents*, February, pp. 2–5. http://files.eric.ed.gov/fulltext/ED118053.pdf (accessed 11 April, 2014).

Simoes, M. (2013). NYU Stern Professor's advice to student: Get your S--- together, *Business Insider*, 11 April.

Simon, N. (2010). *The Participatory Museum*. Santa Cruz, CA: Museum.

Simpson, K. (2005). Dropping out or signing up? The professionalisation of youth travel. In N. Laurie and L. Bondi (Eds.), *Working the Spaces of Neoliberalism: Activism, professionalisation and incorporation* (pp. 54–76). Malden, MA: Blackwell.

Skeggs, B. (2009). The moral economy of person production: the class relations of self-performance on 'reality' television, *The Sociological Review*, 57, 4, 626–644.

Skelton, A. (2005). *Understanding Teaching Excellence in Higher Education: Towards a critical approach*. London: Routledge.

Slade, S. and Prinsloo, P. (2013). Learning analytics: ethical issues and dilemmas, *American Behavioral Scientist*, 57, 10, 1509–1528.

Snyder, B.R. (1971). *The Hidden Curriculum*. New York: Knopf.

Solbrekke, T.D. and Sugrue, C. (2011). Professional responsibility: back to the future. In C. Sugrue and T.D. Solbrekke (Eds.), *Professional Responsibility: New horizons of practice* (pp. 11–28). Oxford: Routledge,

Stark, J.S. (1975). The new consumerism in higher education, *Planning for Higher Education*, 4, 3, 1–5.

Startup, R.A. (1972). How students see the role of university lecturer, *Sociology*, 6, 237–254.

Stefani, L., Mason, R. and Pegler, C. (2007). *The Educational Potential of E-portfolios: Supporting personal development and reflective learning*. Abingdon: Routledge.

Steger, M.B. (2009). *Globalisms*. Lanham, MD, and Oxford: Rowman and Littlefield Publishers Inc.

Stephenson, J. (1993) The student experience of independent study: reaching the parts other programmes appear to miss. In N. Graves (Ed.), *Learner Managed Learning: Practice theory and policy* (pp. 5–22). London and New York: Routledge.

Stevenson, J. and Clegg, S. (2012). Who cares? Gender dynamics in the valuing of extra-curricular activities in higher education, *Gender and Education*, 24, 1, 41–55.

Stewart, S. and Richardson, B. (2000). Reflection and its place in the curriculum on an undergraduate course: should it be assessed? *Assessment & Evaluation in Higher Education*, 25, 4, 369–380.

Sumsion, J. and Fleet, A. (1996). Reflection: can we assess it? Should we assess it?, *Assessment and Evaluation in Higher Education*, 21, 2, 121–130.

Szablewicz, J.J. and Gibbs, A. (1987). Colleges' increasing exposure to liability: the new *in loco parentis*. *Journal of Law and Education*, 16, 4, 453–465.

Thornton, T. (2012). The economics curriculum in Australian universities 1980 to 2011, *Economic Papers: A Journal of Applied Economics and Policy*, 31, 1, 103–113.

Tight, M. (2011). Student accommodation in higher education in the United Kingdom: changing post-war attitudes, *Oxford Review of Education*, 37, 1, 109–122.

Trowler, V. (2010). *Student Engagement Literature Review*. York: The Higher Education Academy. https://www.heacademy.ac.uk/sites/default/files/Student EngagementLiteratureReview_1.pdf (accessed 5 March 2012).

Tucker, B. (2014). Student evaluation surveys: anonymous comments that offend or are unprofessional, *Higher Education*, 68, 3, 347–358.

UNESCO Institute of Statistics (UIS) (2009). *Global Education Digest 2009*. Montreal: UIS (accessed 13 March 2010).

UNESCO Institute of Statistics (UIS) (2012). *Global Education Digest 2012*. Montreal: UIS (accessed 25 October 2013).

UNICEF/UNESCO (2007). *A Human Rights-Based Approach to Education for All*. New York: UNESCO. http://unesdoc.unesco.org/images/0015/001548/154861e.pdf (accessed 2 December 2012).

United Nations (2009). *The Universal Declaration of Human Rights*. http://www.un.org/en/documents/udhr/ (accessed 20 May 2010).

Universities UK (2013). *External Speakers in Higher Education*, Universities UK, London. http://www.universitiesuk.ac.uk/highereducation/Documents/2013/ExternalSpeakersInHigherEducationInstitutions.pdf (accessed 13 February 2014).

University College London (UCL) (2015). *Attendance Requirements: University College London*. https://www.ucl.ac.uk/srs/academic-manual/c1/taught-registration/attendance (accessed 2 December 2015).

University of Alberta (2014). *Global Education Program*. http://www.globaled.ualberta.ca/en/AboutGlobalEducation.aspx (accessed 14 October 2015).

University of Bolton (2011). *Student Attendance Policy*. http://www.bolton.ac.uk/Students/PoliciesProceduresRegulations/AllStudents/Documents/StudentAttendancePolicy.pdf (accessed 20 August 2013).

University of East Anglia (2015). *Student Programme Handbook, 2015–16*. www.uel.ac.uk/.../On-campus-Student-Handbook-2015-16-v.02-July-2015 (accessed 19 September 2015).

University of Hong Kong. (2012). *Common Core*. http://commoncore.hku.hk/global-issues/ (accessed 9 January 2014).

University of Leeds (2011). *Attendance Monitoring: Policy, guidance and examples of good practice for schools*. http://www.leeds.ac.uk/rsa/admissionsandregistration/forstaff/attendance.html (accessed 14 May 2013).

University of Pennsylvania (2012). *Policies Governing Class Attendance (College of Arts and Sciences)*. http://www.college.upenn.edu/class-attendance (accessed 18 November 2012).

Vivian, R., Barnes, A., Geer, R. and Wood, D. (2014). The academic journey of university students on Facebook: an analysis of informal academic-related activity over a semester, *Research in Learning Technology*, 22, 24681.

Volet, S. and Ang, G. (1998). Culturally mixed groups on international campuses: an opportunity for inter-cultural learning, *Higher Education Research and Development*, 17, 1, 5–23.

Vye, C., Scholljegerdes, K. and Welch, I.D. (2007). *Under Pressure and Overwhelmed: Coping with anxiety in college*. Westport, CT: Praeger.

Walker, J. (1998). Student plagiarism in universities: what are we doing about it? *Higher Education Research and Development*, 17, 1, 89–106.

Walker, R.A. (2011). Badgering Big Brother: spectacle, surveillance, and politics in the flash mob, *Liminalities: A Journal of Performance Studies*, 7, 2, 1–23.

Walter, T. (1999). *On Bereavement: The culture of grief.* Oxford: Oxford University Press.

Wang, Y. (2012). Mainland Chinese students' group work adaptation in a UK business school, *Teaching in Higher Education*, 17, 5, 523–535.

Wankowski, J.A. (1973). *Temperament, Motivation, and Academic Achievement: Studies of success and failure of a random sample of students in one university.* Birmingham: University of Birmingham Educational Survey.

Wass, R., Harland, T., McLean, A., Miller, E. and Kwong, N.S. (2015). Will press lever for food: behavioural conditioning of students through frequent high-stakes assessment, *Higher Education Research and Development*, 34, 6, 1324–1326.

Watson, B. (Trans.) (1969). *Records of the Historian: Chapters from the SHIH CHI of Ssu-ma Ch'ien.* New York: Columbia University Press.

Watts, C. and Pickering, A. (2000). Pay as you learn: student employment and academic progress, *Education and Training*, 42, 3, 129–135.

Waugh, W.L. (2003). Issues in university governance: more 'professional' and less academic, *The Annals of the American Academy of Political and Social Science*, 585, 1, 84–96.

Weber, M. (1973a). The academic freedom of the universities (originally published in 1909). In E. Shils (Ed. and Trans.), *Max Weber on Universities: The power of the state and the dignity of the academic calling in Imperial Germany* (pp. 18–23). Chicago and London: University of Chicago Press.

Weber, M. (1973b). The meaning of ethical neutrality in sociology and economics (originally published in 1917). In E. Shils (Ed. and Trans.), *Max Weber on Universities: The power of the state and the dignity of the academic calling in Imperial Germany* (pp. 47–54). Chicago and London: University of Chicago Press.

Williams, P. (2010). Quality assurance: is the jury still out? *The Law Teacher*, 44, 1, 4–16.

Wood, J. (2013). *Transformation Through Journal Writing: The art of self-reflection for the helping professions.* London: Jessica Kingsley.

Zinkin, M. (1967). Galbraith and consumer sovereignty, *The Journal of Industrial Economics*, 16, 1, 1–9.

Index

 Taylor & Francis eBooks

Helping you to choose the right eBooks for your Library

Add Routledge titles to your library's digital collection today. Taylor and Francis ebooks contains over 50,000 titles in the Humanities, Social Sciences, Behavioural Sciences, Built Environment and Law.

Choose from a range of subject packages or create your own!

Benefits for you

» Free MARC records
» COUNTER-compliant usage statistics
» Flexible purchase and pricing options
» All titles DRM-free.

 REQUEST YOUR **FREE** INSTITUTIONAL TRIAL TODAY

Free Trials Available
We offer free trials to qualifying academic, corporate and government customers.

Benefits for your user

» Off-site, anytime access via Athens or referring URL
» Print or copy pages or chapters
» Full content search
» Bookmark, highlight and annotate text
» Access to thousands of pages of quality research at the click of a button.

eCollections – Choose from over 30 subject eCollections, including:

Archaeology	Language Learning
Architecture	Law
Asian Studies	Literature
Business & Management	Media & Communication
Classical Studies	Middle East Studies
Construction	Music
Creative & Media Arts	Philosophy
Criminology & Criminal Justice	Planning
Economics	Politics
Education	Psychology & Mental Health
Energy	Religion
Engineering	Security
English Language & Linguistics	Social Work
Environment & Sustainability	Sociology
Geography	Sport
Health Studies	Theatre & Performance
History	Tourism, Hospitality & Events

For more information, pricing enquiries or to order a free trial, please contact your local sales team:
www.tandfebooks.com/page/sales

 Routledge
Taylor & Francis Group

The home of
Routledge books

www.tandfebooks.com